Wool, Needle & Thread

THE GO-TO GUIDE FOR WOOL STITCHERY

Lisa Bongean of Primitive Gatherings

Wool, Needle & Thread: The Go-To Guide for Wool Stitchery
© 2019 by Lisa Bongean

Martingale®
19021 120th Ave. NE, Ste. 102
Bothell, WA 98011-9511 USA
ShopMartingale.com

Printed in China
24 23 22 21 20 19   8 7 6 5 4 3 2 1

Library of Congress Cataloging-in-Publication Data is available upon request.

ISBN: 978-1-68356-031-9

MISSION STATEMENT

We empower makers who use fabric and yarn to make life more enjoyable.

CREDITS

**PUBLISHER AND
CHIEF VISIONARY OFFICER**
Jennifer Erbe Keltner

CONTENT DIRECTOR
Karen Costello Soltys

DESIGN MANAGER
Adrienne Smitke

MANAGING EDITOR
Tina Cook

PRODUCTION MANAGER
Regina Girard

**ACQUISITIONS AND
DEVELOPMENT EDITOR**
Laurie Baker

PHOTOGRAPHER
Adam Albright

COPY EDITOR
Sheila Chapman Ryan

ILLUSTRATOR
Sandy Loi

CONTENTS

INTRODUCTION

As a stitcher, a pattern and fabric designer, and a shop owner, I feel blessed every day to do what I do for a living. I put a little piece of my heart into each and every project I create.

This book is a compilation of techniques that I've honed in more than twenty years of experience hand stitching with wool. There's almost nothing (other than my family) that gives me more joy than teaching stitchers, young and old, how to make these stitches more easily, more consistently, and more beautifully. Why? Because when your needle glides in and out of the wool and those gorgeous stitches embellish your project just right, the whole experience becomes more enjoyable and more relaxing. Who doesn't want an activity that does that?

As we took the photographs and wrote the text and tips for this book, my goal was for these pages to be the nearest thing to being in a class with me. Those are my hands you see in the pictures. And it's my advice for what to do (or in some cases what not to do) to get the finished stitches just right. It's all my wool stitchery tips and tricks in one easy-to-find place!

I share with you the tools that I find useful and the reasons why. You'll learn the techniques needed to begin and end a project. And my favorite section is the stitches with detailed step-by-step photos. It's as if you're looking over my shoulder at exactly how they're done.

There are lots of unfinished projects in the world. Most often, I think a lack of confidence or skill stops people from seeing things through to the end. I hope the techniques in the book give you the courage to complete your projects. And once you complete one, I hope you're so happy with the results that you can't wait to begin another project right away. Let's stitch!

SUPPLIES

Very few supplies are needed for stitching on wool.
However, as you become more and more addicted to it
(and you will, believe me), you may find your wool and
thread collection growing. What can I say? It happens.

Felted Wool

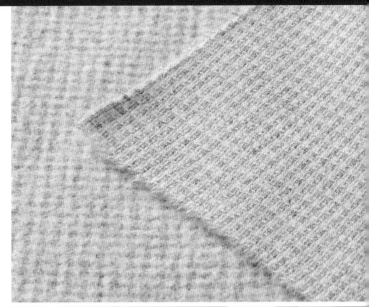

The wool fabric you use for appliqué must be felted, otherwise the edges of the shapes will ravel endlessly as you try to stitch them in place. Wool can be purchased already felted, or you can buy unfelted wool and felt it yourself.

My wool of choice is 100% wool. You can tell by looking at this pair of fabrics (above right) that the unfelted fabric on top has a looser weave than the fabric on bottom, which is felted and has a fuzzier texture. If you could feel them, you'd also notice that the felted wool is thicker than the unfelted wool.

Hand-dyed wools are boiled during the dying process, which felts them at the same time, so you never have to worry about knowing if a hand-dyed wool is felted or not. The dying process also gives wool a mottled coloration throughout (middle right). Between the tightly woven finish, the subtle variations in color, and the unlimited color palette, what's not to love about hand-dyed wool?

All of the wool included in any Primitive Gatherings kit (below right) has been felted and is ready to stitch, but don't assume every shop uses wool that's already been felted; ask if you're not sure. My shops often lay out the wool in the kits in the order they're called for in the materials as well, especially when there might be several fabrics from the same color family.

Kits can be an economical choice because you don't need a hefty stash to create a colorful project. And if you love a scrappy look, kits are a great way to incorporate a variety of colors and textures without buying a lot of yardage.

Double-Sided Fusible Web

shapes will sometimes pop off the background fabric while I'm stitching. Trying to find a missing piece isn't fun when I'm in the stitching groove or traveling and don't have access to all my fabrics to replace a lost piece.

The key to a good bond is the STEAM. Lite Steam-A-Seam 2 needs a generous amount of steam. Most people are too timid to use steam on wool. With unfelted wool, steam might be a problem. But felted wool and steam are best friends. You can't wreck a piece of felted wool with steam. Once the shapes are fused in place, I can travel with projects and not worry about losing an appliqué shape.

Lite Steam-a-Seam 2 comes packaged in 9" x 12" sheets and on 12"-, 18"-, and 24"-wide rolls that can be cut to the desired length. Do not follow the instructions that come with the product; they're written primarily for cotton fabrics. Instead, refer to "Prepare the Appliqué Shapes" (page 20) and "Fuse the Appliqués" (page 24) or the instructions that come with any Primitive Gatherings wool pattern.

I'm often asked why I use a fusible product with wool appliqué. The reason I use a double-sided fusible is easy—regardless of what method you're using, the design has to be traced. Instead of using freezer paper, fusible web gives you the benefit of being adhesive. Your pieces stay where you place them. You can temporarily stick the shape to the background fabric, move it around if you need to, and then fuse it in place when you're ready. I also like the clean edges; using fusible controls the fuzziness of the wool at the edges by keeping the fibers in place.

Lite Steam-a-Seam 2 (above) is my favorite double-sided fusible web because it bonds securely. Other brands lack the stickiness needed, and wool

KEEPING THE FRAY AT BAY

Some wools have a looser weave and the fibers separate even after the fabric has been felted and the appliqué has been fused in place. This happens rarely but primarily with textured wools such as those with a check, houndstooth, or herringbone pattern woven into the fabric. To prevent any further loosening of the fibers, I apply a miniscule amount of Fray Check (shown at left in the photo above left) to the appliqué edges before stitching.

Marking Tools and Templates

I keep several marking tools on hand for different tasks.

Clover white marking pen. For marking any lines that will be stitched on medium- and dark-colored wools, I use a Clover fine-tip white marking pen. The marking substance is actually liquid chalk, but it won't rub off like dry chalk; you have to steam it off. Use a light touch when marking with this pen; the mark doesn't show up immediately, so many people tend to press harder, but don't. The liquid gets darker as it dries, so be patient.

FriXion pen. To mark lines that will be stitched on light-colored wool, I use FriXion pens. Marks made with FriXion pens can be erased with heat. They come in a variety of colors and styles, and I like to match the ink color to the thread color I'll be using. If I'm doing redwork, I use a red pen. If I'm marking stems and leaves, I use a green pen. The marks come back with extreme cold, so you want to make sure any marks you make will be stitched over.

TRACING PERFECT CIRCLES

I'm a firm believer that if you want a perfect finished circle, you have to trace a perfect circle first . . . and that's not easy when you're tracing from a pattern. My solution is to use a circle template, and my favorite is a template that contains many circle sizes (shown in the photo above left). I use my Sharpie marker to trace the size I need.

Sharpie. My tool of choice for tracing patterns onto fusible web is an ultra-fine-point Sharpie marker. Finer lines create more accurate shapes, and the ink dries quickly, so there's less chance of smudged lines. For accuracy in shapes, try to trace on the line rather than next to it.

Threads and Needles

*Pair a #24 chenille needle (left) with either a single strand of three-strand floss or
#12 pearl cotton. Use a #22 chenille needle (right) with either #5 or #8 pearl cotton.*

Thread is sized by weight—the larger the number, the finer the thread. I typically use four weights of thread when stitching on wool: #5 pearl cotton, #8 pearl cotton, #12 pearl cotton, and three-strand floss (which can be separated into single strands for a finer stitch). The thread weight I use depends on the size of the appliqué shape. Sometimes I want the thread to be the star, and sometimes I want the wool to be the star, with thread taking the supporting role.

I prefer using hand-dyed Valdani pearl cotton and floss in my work. Valdani threads have a wide range of colors that complement my hand-dyed wool fabrics, and they're a little thicker than other brands.

Hand-sewing needles are sized like thread— the larger the number, the finer the needle. Primitive Gatherings carries every type of needle you'll need for stitching on wool. Each tube of needles is labeled with the needle size and intended use, so you won't forget what they're for (page 11).

- **Pincushion/doll needles.** The extra-long 4" length helps you stitch through a thick pincushion.

- **Embellishment needles.** The shaft and eye are the same width the entire length of the needle. The longer length is perfect for making bullion and drizzle stitches.

- **Basting needles.** These long, sturdy needles aren't too thick; they glide nicely through the layers.

- **Size 22 and 24 chenille needles.** These are the primary needles I use for stitching on wool. Our chenille needles are sharper and shorter than other brands, making them easier to work with.

- **Big-stitch needles.** These are similar to a Between quilting needle but the eye is larger to accommodate pearl cotton.

- **Binding needles.** These are fine but sturdy at the same time, similar to a straw needle, but they don't bend and the eye is larger for easier threading.

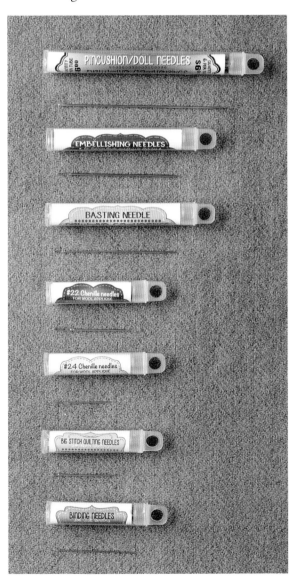

If you struggle to thread needles, try using the LoRan Needle Threader. This little gem is great to use with pearl cotton. Just slide your needle eye over the hook, then hook your thread (below top). Pull the eye back over the hook (below middle) to thread . . . easy as 1-2-3! I have one in all my project cases, so I'm never without it.

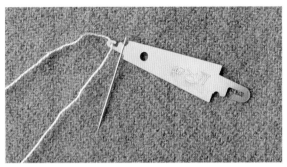

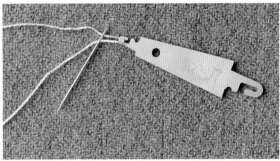

Struggling to keep track of which thread colors you own in which weights? *My Soul Is Fed with My Wool, Needle & Thread* is a little Primitive Gatherings booklet (below) you can use to keep track of your Valdani threads.

Cutting Tools, Tweezers, and Rulers

Trimming, cutting, measuring, and placing pieces are all part of the wool-stitching process, and having the right tools makes everything easier and more accurate.

Good scissors are essential when cutting through the thickness of felted wool. German-made Dovo scissors are my favorite. They're high-end heirloom quality scissors, and worth the investment. Scissors are really a personal preference based on individual comfort, so try out different pairs before buying. Consider how they feel in your hand, the comfort of the finger holes, and the cutting action. I suggest having a small pair of embroidery scissors for snipping threads and a 5" or 6" pair of scissors for cutting fabric.

I use a 60 mm rotary cutter for cutting straight lines on patterns and trimming long fabric edges and an 18 mm rotary cutter for cutting fusible web before it's adhered to wool. The small 18 mm cutter is easy on my hands, and I can make tighter turns and cut faster and more efficiently than with scissors.

Fine-tipped tweezers are helpful for removing fusible-web paper from the back of appliqués and

also when placing appliqués on the background fabric, especially for tiny pieces like berries.

I use rulers for specific tasks, such as cutting straight lines and trimming straight edges. My favorites are the Itty Bitty series of rulers I designed for Creative Grids. These rulers feature easy-to-read black and white dashed lines in ⅛" increments. You can see the lines at any point and on any fabric color.

I also created two Primitive Gatherings Stem rulers (3" × 8" and 3" × 16") specifically for cutting stems (above right). I like the look of a ¼"-wide stem, but if you cut a wool ¼" stem, by the time you stitch it, it's stretched and looks larger. To avoid that, I cut ³⁄₁₆"-wide stems. By the time I add stitching and the wool fluffs up, it's a true ¼". Cutting *on* the marked line rather than *inside* it also makes a difference. You can do this with any ruler, but it's much more convenient to follow the ³⁄₁₆" line on the Stem ruler. See "Make Stems" (page 22) for using Stem rulers.

Pressing Tools

For my wool-appliqué method, it's essential to have a good steam iron with a wool setting. Steam protects the wool so it doesn't scorch and is necessary to properly adhere the fusible web to the wool fibers. The more steam the iron produces, the better. And the more steam holes in the iron's soleplate, the better! The standard 12-hole iron doesn't cut it; more holes means better steam distribution.

I like a tank iron so I don't have to refill the water reservoir as often as a regular iron. My iron of choice is the Rowenta Perfect Steam Station with the Microsteam 400 soleplate (right), which produces massive amounts of steam that is evenly distributed because of all the holes in the soleplate.

A pressing mat made from 100% wool is fabulous for any type of patchwork pressing you do and is the absolute best for adhering fusible web to wool. Why? Because the mat holds the heat and steam from the iron and pushes it back up into the piece, essentially pressing it from both sides at once. Without it, when you're working on a regular ironing board, the steam passes through your piece and then through the ironing surface.

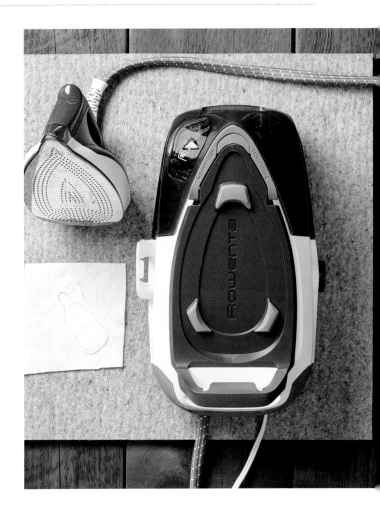

CARE FOR YOUR IRON

Following the manufacturer's instructions, clean and maintain your iron often. It will last longer if you do.

TECHNIQUES

Before you can begin stitching, you'll need to prepare the various pieces of your project. For some projects, you can prepare your background for fusing to a backing piece later; for others, it's simply a matter of cutting out the background. All Primitive Gatherings appliqué patterns, including the ones in this book, have already been reversed, so they're ready for tracing. If you're using these techniques for another appliqué pattern, you may need to reverse the pattern piece before tracing them onto the double-sided fusible web. A light box or sunny window can make it easier to see the lines.

It might seem silly to include instructions for threading a needle, knotting the thread end, and finding the thread end on a ball of pearl cotton, but I've been stitching for a long time and have learned some nifty tricks along the way that make things easier—and my students agree! So, before you skip over this section, just take a minute and give my methods a try. Stitching should be enjoyable, so if these techniques don't work for you, use what does.

Prepare the Appliqué Background

Follow these steps when making a table mat, penny rug, or other project where the appliqué background is later fused to a backing. This technique lets you later finish the edges with blanket stitching rather than binding. (To learn more about that finishing method, turn to page 30.)

1 Before you begin, note whether your pattern is designed for fusible appliqué. All Primitive Gatherings patterns/shapes are reversed for fusible. If you're using a different pattern that is NOT designed for fusible web, you'll need to reverse the shapes before tracing. If you're working on a dark surface, place a blank sheet of white paper beneath your pattern to help with visibility of lines.

Trace the full-size background pattern onto the gridded side of the fusible web using an ultra-fine-tip Sharpie (1). Try to trace directly on the line. Add some registration marks—AA, BB, CC, DD, etc.—inside the traced shape. Place one letter right next to the traced line and the other about 1" above it, making sure both letters are *inside* the shape. These marks will be helpful to you later.

2 Using an 18 mm rotary cutter, roughly cut out the shape approximately ⅛" *outside* the drawn line (2). If the fusible web tries to pull away and go to the nongridded side of the paper, gently pull it back onto the gridded side of the paper. Always rough cut fusible web. Never cut it on the line unless it's already adhered to the wool.

3 Cut ½" to ¾" *inside* the drawn line, cutting between the matching registration letters you previously marked (3a). Remove the cutout center piece of fusible web and set it aside, but DON'T throw it away or crumple it! You'll need this piece later to make sure your background maintains its shape. The remaining outer ring will be fused to the background wrong side (3b).

4 Steam the wool background fabric flat (4).

5 Slowly peel the paper off the back (non-gridded side) of the outer ring of your fusible-web traced pattern (5). Make sure the fusible layer stays with the gridded paper side you traced on. Be gentle at this stage; the fusible can begin to separate from the paper if you pull it apart too quickly.

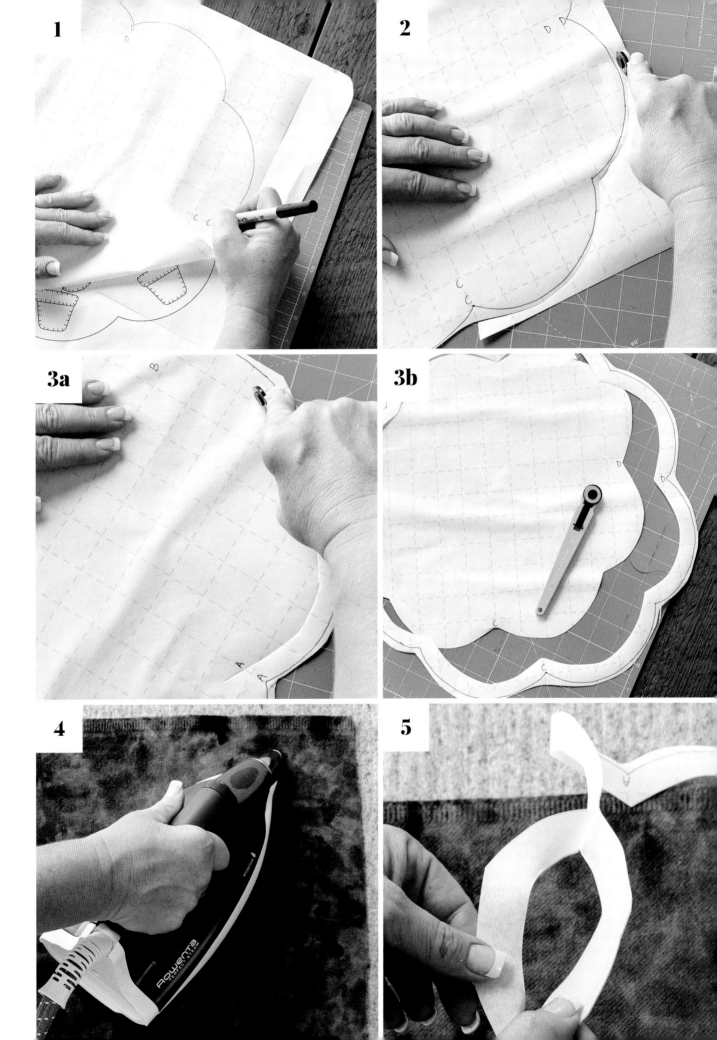

1

2

3a

3b

4

5

6 With the gridded side up, position the cutout center of your fusible pattern that you previously set aside in step 3 onto the wrong side of your wool background (6). (Yes, wool is usually the same on both sides, but you may like one side better than the other.) DO NOT REMOVE THE PAPER OR FUSE this center piece; you'll use it later to trace additional patterns.

7 With the tacky side down, gently place the fusible-web outer ring around the center piece, aligning the registration letters (7). Fusible web has a tackiness to it that helps keep the original shape in place. Positioning it in this manner will help ensure that the finished shape matches the original shape you traced. Once everything fits properly, pat the ring in place to temporarily hold it on the background fabric.

8 Remove the fusible-web center piece and set it aside. Using a *dry* iron set on the wool setting (there is no need to use steam on paper), press the traced pattern onto the wool background (8). Always keep your iron moving, using up and down motions, and don't press so hard that the pattern piece shifts. Go slow enough that the fusible adheres. Don't worry about pressing Lite Steam-a-Seam 2 too much; it can take the heat.

9 Use scissors to cut out the background piece on the drawn line. Use long strokes, not short, choppy ones (9).

10 When you're finished cutting out the background, do not remove the paper on the fusible (10). It will remain in place until after all the appliqués have been stitched in place.

Set the background aside and we'll proceed to prepare the appliqué shapes (page 20).

DO IT YOUR WAY

If the paper on your fusible outer ring starts coming off during stitching, you can remove it (but you will not be able to iron your project until the stitching is completely finished), or you can baste it in place with pearl cotton to hold it together.

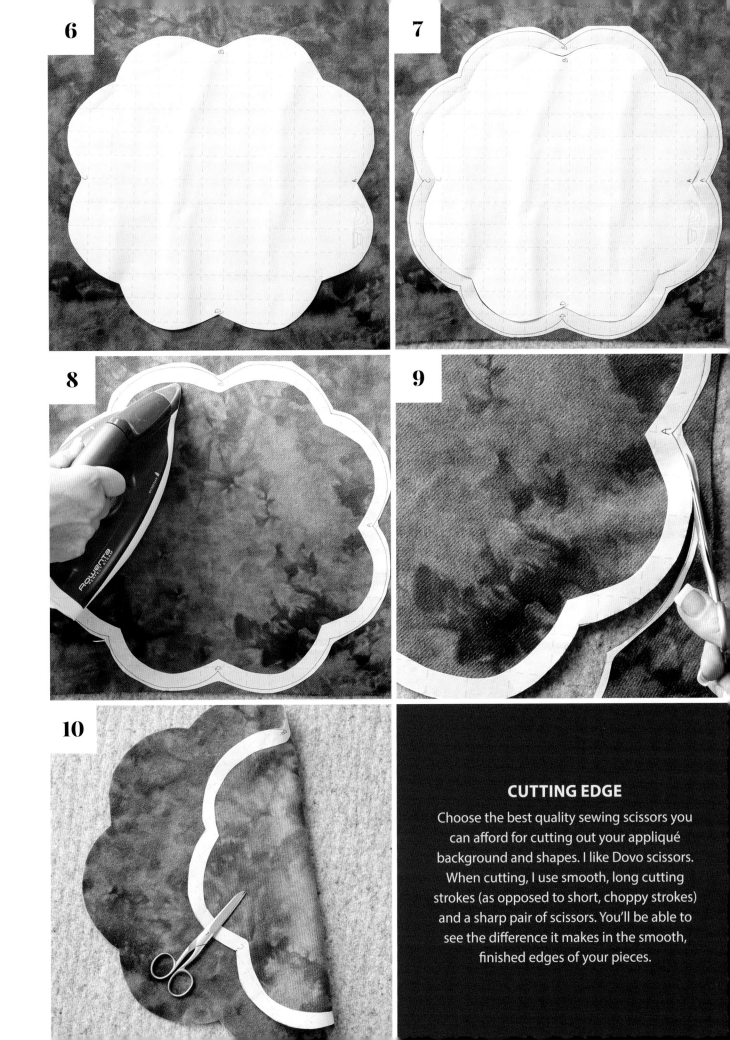

6

7

8

9

10

CUTTING EDGE

Choose the best quality sewing scissors you can afford for cutting out your appliqué background and shapes. I like Dovo scissors. When cutting, I use smooth, long cutting strokes (as opposed to short, choppy strokes) and a sharp pair of scissors. You'll be able to see the difference it makes in the smooth, finished edges of your pieces.

Prepare the Appliqué Shapes

If you first prepared a background piece (page 16), work with the remaining cutout center piece of double-sided fusible web first. If not, the process is the same but you'll be working with the fusible-web piece called for in the project materials.

1 Working with the wool pieces from your kit or the pieces called for in the project's materials list, place the largest piece of wool that will be used for the appliqués on the gridded side of the fusible web. Lightly mark the perimeter of the wool (1) to make sure the appliqué shapes will fit the wool piece. I've done this often enough that I just trace around the corners, but you might want to start by marking the full length of the sides.

2 Trace all of the appliqué shapes for the corresponding wool fabric onto the fusible web within the perimeter lines you've drawn (2). This makes the most efficient use of your fusible web, wool, and time. There's no need to leave any space between the drawn shapes because there's no seam allowance on these pieces.

3 Roughly cut out the ENTIRE GROUP of shapes approximately ⅛" from the perimeter of the traced pieces (3); this will not necessarily match the perimeter of the wool you drew.

4 Carefully peel off the paper backing (4a) to expose the tacky side of the fusible web. Make sure the fusible layer stays with the gridded paper side you traced on. Position the web on the wool piece (4b). Do NOT press yet!

Repeat all steps to trace the remaining appliqué shapes. To be most efficient, everything that shares the same wool color should be traced together at once.

5 With a *dry* iron (remember, no steam on paper), press the traced pieces onto their corresponding wool pieces (5). The fusible-web paper will have a grayish cast once it adheres to the wool; this is normal, so don't be alarmed.

The extra wool can be used in other projects. Save the scraps for simple pincushions and such.

6 Cut out all the fusible shapes, cutting on or just inside the line (6). As I'm cutting, I keep my scissor blades perpendicular to the wool. Because wool has a thickness to it and I don't want to bevel the edge, I keep my scissors stationary and rotate the wool with my other hand to trim around the shapes. High-quality scissors make it easier to accomplish clean, crisp cuts on your wool, even on small shapes.

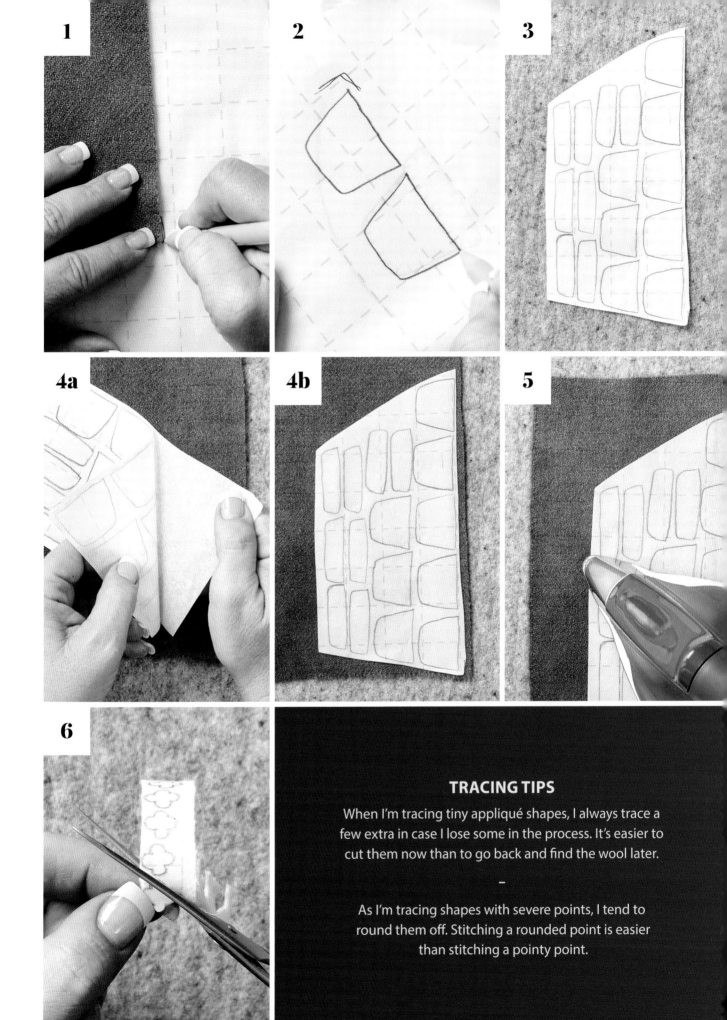

1

2

3

4a

4b

5

6

TRACING TIPS

When I'm tracing tiny appliqué shapes, I always trace a few extra in case I lose some in the process. It's easier to cut them now than to go back and find the wool later.

–

As I'm tracing shapes with severe points, I tend to round them off. Stitching a rounded point is easier than stitching a pointy point.

Make Stems

Stems cut ¼" wide never result in ¼"-wide stems. They always get too chubby as the wool expands. This method uses the Primitive Gatherings Stem ruler to cut ³⁄₁₆" stems that result in perfect ¼" stems. Two sizes of the Stem ruler are available: 3" × 8" and 3" × 16".

1 Cut a piece of double-sided fusible web slightly smaller than the wool piece you're using for the stems. Fuse it to the wrong side of the wool (1).

2 With the paper side up, trim off the long left-hand edge of the wool, like you would do to square up the edge of cotton fabric for piecing (2).

3 Line up the line on the Stem ruler that corresponds to the number of stems you need to cut with the straightened left-hand edge of the fabric (3). For instance, if the pattern calls for seven stems, line up the straightened edge with the 7 line on the Stem ruler. The ruler has notations for right-handed and left-handed people. Pay attention to those notations. I'm right-handed, so I'm using the numbers on the right-handed end.

4 Trim away the excess fabric along the right-hand edge of the ruler with the rotary cutter (4).

5 Move the ruler so the left edge of the wool is now aligned with the 6 line and trim along the right-hand edge of the ruler to create one ³⁄₁₆" stem (5a). To cut the next stem, slide the ruler to the left so the left edge of the wool is aligned with the 5 line; trim along the right-hand edge of the ruler. Continue in this manner to cut all seven stems (5b).

KEEP A STASH OF STEMS

If the wool provided is generous, I cut extra stems to be used in other projects. It's handy to have stems ready to go when you need something quick.

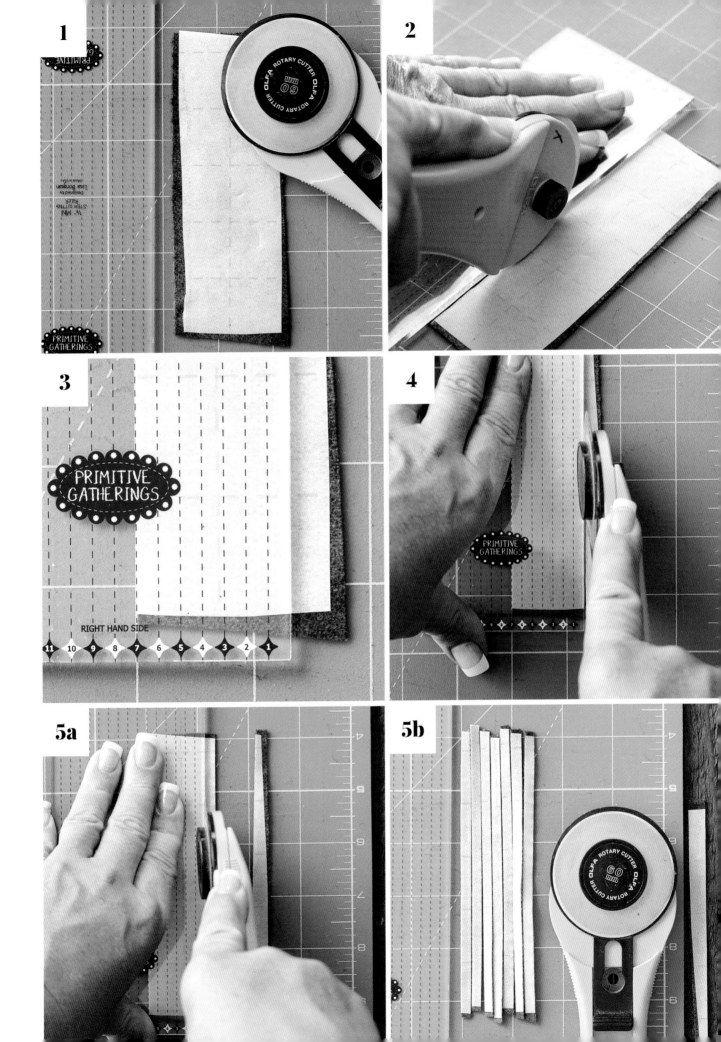

1

2

3

PRIMITIVE
GATHERINGS

RIGHT HAND SIDE

11 10 9 8 7 6 5 4 3 2 1

4

PRIMITIVE
GATHERINGS

5a

5b

Fuse the Appliqués

Follow these steps to fuse the appliqués to the background.

1 Fine-tipped tweezers are your friends when it comes to itty-bitty appliqué pieces. I use mine to pick up tiny pieces by stabbing them with the tips (1a) and also to remove paper backings (1b). Finally, I use them to place the shapes in their final location (1c).

2 When removing the paper backing from larger shapes, I use the tips of my scissors to score the paper in the center of the piece (2a). Then I peel away the paper from the scored area, rather than peeling it away from the edge (2b). Pulling from the edge or a corner can ruffle the edge of an appliqué. This is a simple way to alleviate the problem.

3 For smaller shapes, hold the shape in your nondominant hand with the paper side up. Fold over a corner of the appliqué enough so that the paper touches paper (3a). Press the folded corner between your fingers and make a motion as if you're snapping your fingers. This maneuver helps create enough friction to loosen the paper from the fusible adhered to the wool (3b). Grab the folded corner and pull off the paper (3c).

4 Begin positioning the appliqués on the right side of the background in the order outlined in the pattern instructions (4). Remove the paper right before you place each piece. In this example, the pot is placed first, then the petals are placed in the vicinity of the yet-to-be-stitched stem.

5 Once all the appliqués are in place, it's time to turn on the steam. Set your iron on the highest wool setting. Position the soleplate of the iron directly above the appliqués you're fusing and place it squarely on top of them (5a). Using MAXIMUM STEAM and moving the iron up and down, fuse the layers together. Sometimes I do a quick prepress and check to make sure nothing has adhered to the iron (oops, did I position something upside down?). If it's all good, I repeat with additional pressure (5b).

1a

1b

1c

2a

2b

3a

3b

3c

TIMELY TRIMMING

If you see any stray threads coming off your appliqué shapes, trim them off with scissors as you go, before adhering the pieces to the background.

4

5a

5b

Finding the End of a Thread Ball

Using a ball of thread and having a problem finding the end? Follow these steps.

1 Roll the thread ball in your hand until you find what looks like the outermost wind of the thread (1).

2 Place the tip of your needle underneath a single thread of the outermost wind (2).

3 Pull that one thread to the side of the ball so it begins to unwind (3a), freeing the tail (3b).

Threading a Needle

Ever struggle to get thread through the eye of your needle? Try my threading method.

1 This technique is dependent on having the right size needle eye for your thread. It does make a difference! Loop the thread over your forefinger (4).

2 Place the eye of the needle dead center onto the thread near the side of your finger; let go of everything but the needle holding the thread (5). This is very important.

3 Press down on the needle as you roll your forefinger away from yourself (6a), which will force the thread into the needle's eye (6b).

4 Pull the thread through the needle's eye (7).

IT'S A MATCH!

THREAD WEIGHT	CHENILLE NEEDLE SIZE
#5 pearl cotton	#22
#8 pearl cotton	#22
#12 pearl cotton	#24
3-strand floss	#24

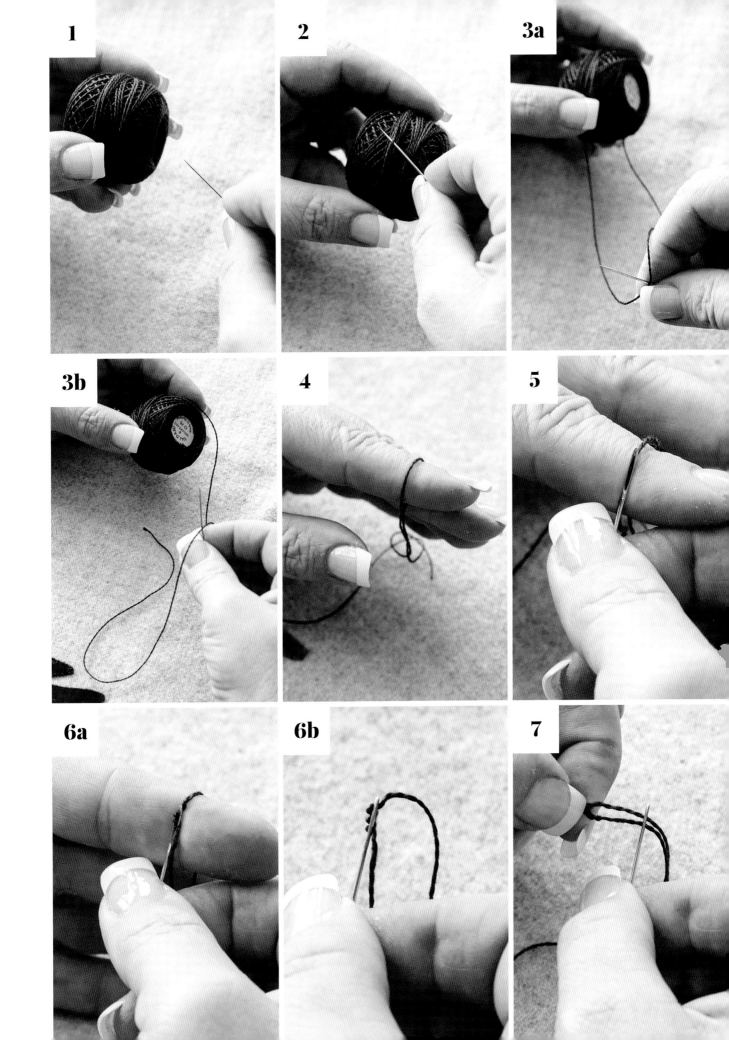

Knotting the End of the Thread

Follow these steps to knot your thread tail before you stitch.

1 Once your needle is threaded, cross the tail end of the thread over the needle at the place on the thread where you want the knot to end up (1). I call this "Make a cross and pray it works."

2 With your dominant hand holding both the needle and the thread tail, place your thumb on the thread tail to hold it in place on the needle (2).

3 Wrap the working end of the thread (the long end, not the tail end) behind the needle (3a), and continue wrapping it clockwise around the tip, making three wraps (3b). Three wraps is the average number; you can make more or fewer depending on how big you want the knot.

4 Pull the wrapped working thread down between your thumb and forefinger (the ones holding the needle in your dominant hand; 4).

5 Now, gently pull the needle up, keeping the knot between your fingers but sliding the needle up and away (5).

6 Use your middle finger on the nondominant hand to prevent the thread from sliding out of the eye of the needle (6).

7 Continue pulling the needle until the knot is tight (7a). Your knot is complete (7b).

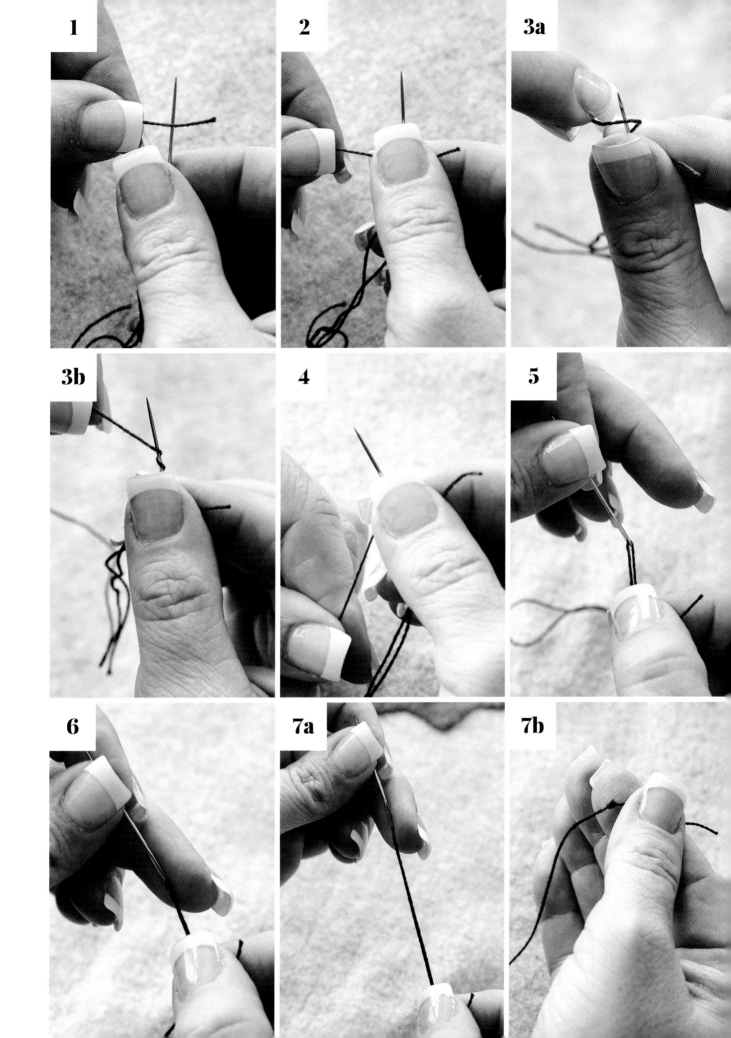

Finishing the Project Edge

When I'm not binding a finished project, this is my go-to finishing method for all my wool mats—round, scalloped, oval, or anything in between. (Refer to "Prepare the Appliqué Background" on page 16, then follow these instructions to finish your project.)

1 After your project is completely stitched, press it one final time. Select a backing fabric, preferably a homespun or brushed woven that looks the same on both sides. Brushed woven fabrics are a good choice in keeping with the fuzzy look of wool. Try to match your backing fabric to the tones of the wool background (1).

2 Iron out any wrinkles from your backing fabric. Remove the paper backing from the fusible web on the back of your finished project (2).

3 With *wrong* sides together, position your project on the backing fabric (3). If you're working with a brushed fabric, the brushed side is the right side. If the project is large, smooth out any excess fabric or wrinkles so the mat lies flat, working from the center out toward the edge.

4 Using your iron, press from the center out using lots of steam (4). Lift the iron up and down, going first from the center toward the top, then from the center toward the bottom. Continue pressing from the center to the left, and then from the center to the right. Press any remaining areas not yet touched by the iron.

5 Finish pressing by concentrating on the outer edge where the rim of fusible web is. Flip the project over and press the back side as well. Let cool. Cut away the background fabric with sharp scissors, cutting right along the edge of the wool (5).

6 After you've cut around the entire project, apply a tiny line of Fray Check along the edge of the backing to prevent any stray threads (6). How thin a line? You only want the opening of the Fray Check bottle to be the width of a pin. (See "Pinhole Tip" on page 32).

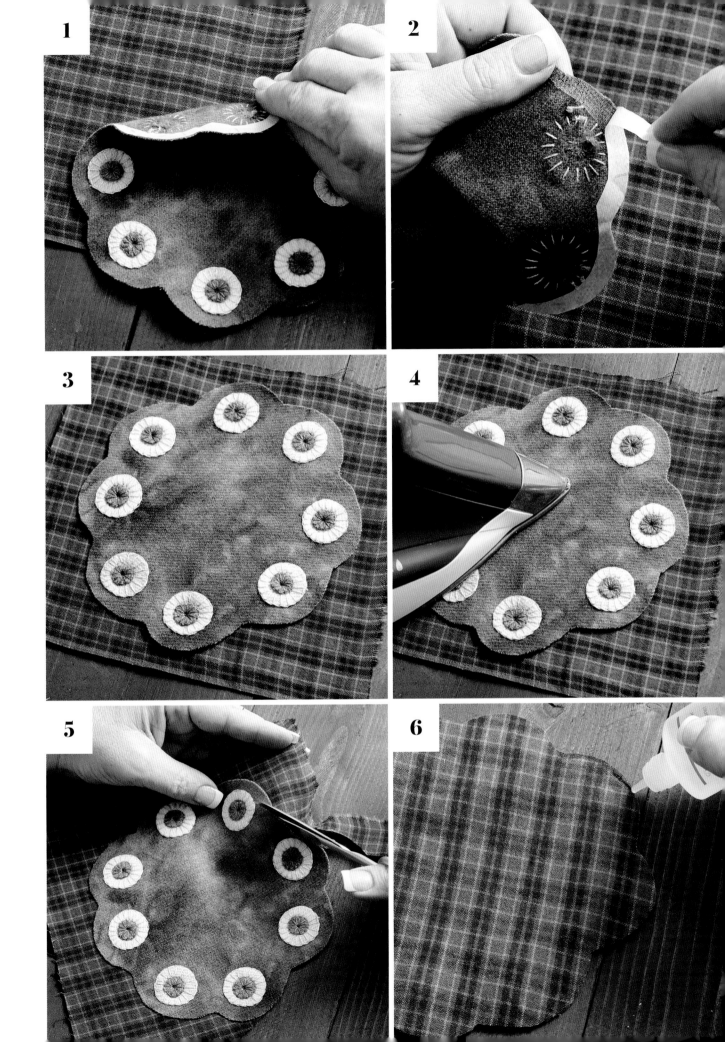

7 Thread your needle but do not knot the end. Insert the needle from the top of the project, 1" from where you want to begin stitching (7). I always use a size 22 needle and either #8 or #5 thread on the edge. The thread used for these photos is #8.

8 Bring out the needle tip between the layers along the edge of the project (8). Do not pull the thread through yet. (The fusible web along the edges is what will ultimately hold the thread tail in place.)

9 Pull the thread through so just a short, unknotted thread tail remains on the front of the mat (9).

10 Rotate your working thread counterclockwise to make a C and insert the needle straight below where the thread emerges from the mat edge (10a). The needle is going in perpendicular to the mat edge, straight through to the backing, not coming out between the layers (10b).

11 Loop the thread behind the needle (11).

12 Hold tension on the working thread to the left with your nondominant hand while you pull the needle through the fabric (12).

13 Pull the thread taut so it gently rests on the edge, completing the first stitch (13).

PINHOLE TIP

If you hold the bottle of Fray Check up to the light, you can see where to cut off the tip so you can use the product. I cut mine just above where the closed tip ends, and then poke a heavy-duty quilting pin through the tip so that I have just a tiny opening.

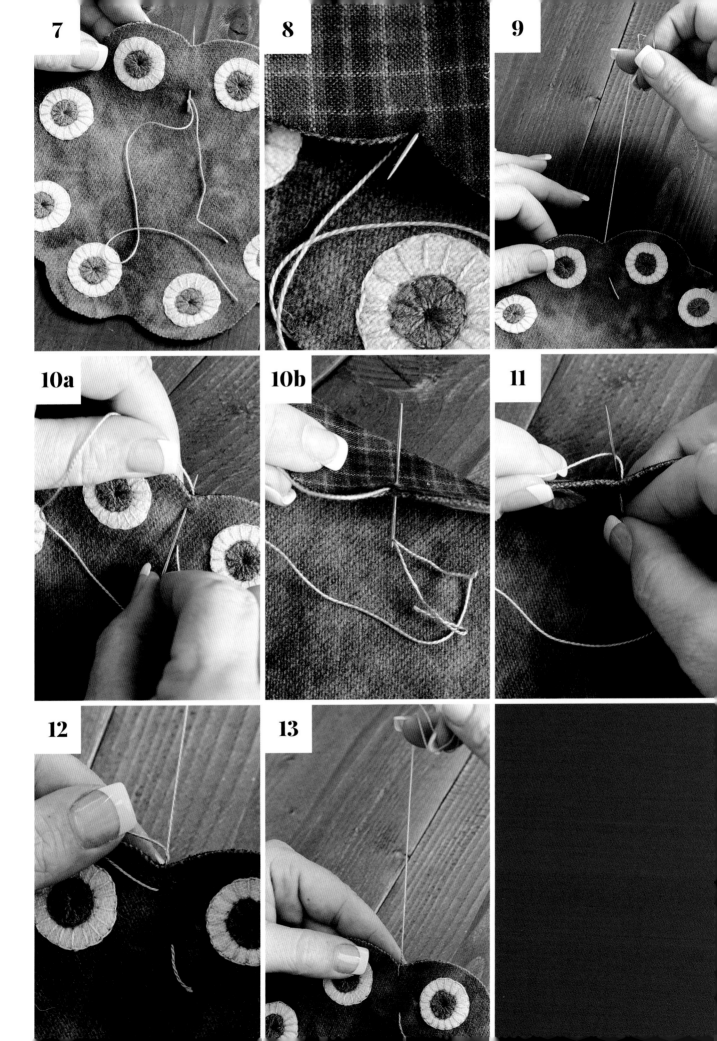

14 Work counterclockwise and lay the thread along the edge of the mat, approximately ¼" from the first stitch. Again, positioning your needle to go through the mat perpendicular to the mat edge, stab your needle through both layers, wrapping the working thread under the needle (14).

15 Pull the needle through to form the next stitch (15a). The edge of the blanket stitch should lie flat along the raw edge of the mat. Continue stitching around the mat (15b).

16 When you need to end a thread, stop with about 4" of thread remaining, and circle the thread counterclockwise as if you were going to start another stitch. Instead, insert your needle from the back through the edge and bite through the wool just into the corner of the last blanket stitch (16).

17 Pull your needle through the fabric, making a small loop with the thread (17).

18 Insert the needle once through the loop, and then pull taut while holding the needle perpendicular to the edge to make a tiny knot (18). For these photos, we've used contrasting thread so you can see the stitches, but normally the thread would match the wool background color and the knot wouldn't be visible.

19 Reinsert the needle into the edge of the mat between the layers, as close as you can get to the knot, and come out about 1" away from the edge in the backing only (19a). Push the needle through, checking to make sure your needle didn't pierce the front of your mat. Clip the excess thread, leaving about an inch or so showing (19b). The tail will be clipped later.

20 To begin a new thread, repeat the starting thread process, bringing your needle tip out along the edge just next to the last completed blanket stitch. The knot you made in step 19 will be just to the left of where your needle emerges (20). Pull the needle through, leaving a tail as before.

RELEASING THE THREAD

During stitching, always keep your middle finger on the eye of the needle to keep the thread length consistent. Lift your finger to release more thread.

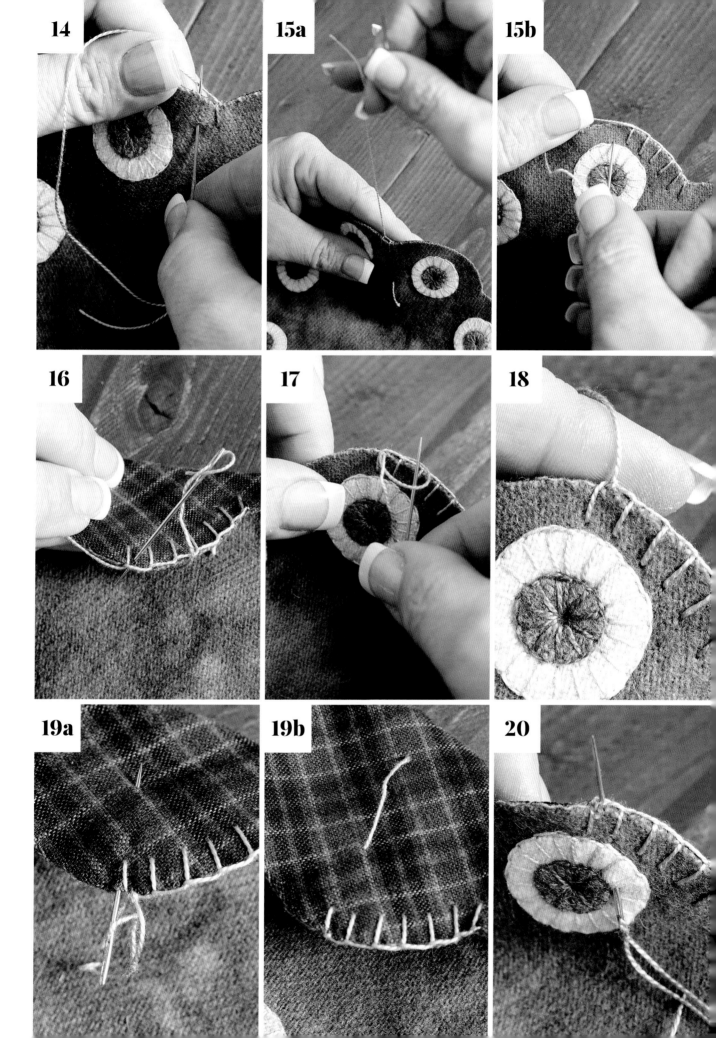

21 Hold the working thread with your non-stitching hand and insert the needle into the edge to begin stitching again. On the first stitch at the beginning of the mat, the needle went straight down; on restart, that stitch is already formed, so move the needle over ¼" from the last stitch before you insert it (21). You'll still position your needle stab perpendicular to the mat and your working thread along the edge of the mat.

22 Wrap the thread behind the needle and pull it through as before (22). Continue stitching around the entire project, starting and stopping as previously described. To end, knot the last thread on the edge, joining it to the starting point.

23 Before you clip any thread tails, steam your mat again. Doing so will reactivate the fusible web to capture the thread tails in it, holding them securely between the wool mat and backing edges. The beginning thread tails are on the front of the mat; the ending of the thread tails are on the back.

24 To clip thread tails, pull up on a tail slightly. Place your scissors parallel to the mat at the base of the tail and snip (23). By holding the scissors this way, you won't clip your mat accidentally. Repeat to clip all the tails on the front and back (24).

21

22

23

24

MATCHING THREADS

The step-by-step photos show contrasting thread so it's easier to see and demonstrate the stitches. But for almost all the stitches I do, I try to use matching thread as in the project shown at right.

Connecting Penny Shapes

Pennies are a classic shape in wool stitchery. But connecting them can be tricky unless you know the secrets to success. They're all here for you!

1 Lay out your pennies in the desired arrangement. Using a liquid chalk pen (the marks will eventually steam away), mark a straight line at each point where the pennies meet (1). The marked lines will be the stitching points where the pennies will be joined.

2 Pick up the center penny of your design; note the location of the marked white line (2). Pick up the adjacent penny whose marked line touches the noted line location. Place them right sides together with the marks aligned.

3 Insert your threaded needle approximately ¾" away from the edge of the penny closest to you and bring the tip out between the backing and front edge of that same penny at the marking (3), leaving a tail. (Use thread that matches the penny background; we used contrasting thread in these photos for easier visibility.)

4 Swing the thread counterclockwise in a C shape and insert the needle perpendicular to the edge through both pennies, a scant ⅛" from the edge at the marked lines (4).

5 Pull your needle through both pennies (5a), and then pull it taut (5b). This will join the two pennies. Do not pull the thread tail through.

6 Loop the thread counterclockwise again and insert the needle at the exact same spot (making a tacking stitch), but don't pull it taut (6). Instead, leave a loop.

7 Circle the thread counterclockwise with the needle and put the needle through the thread loop only (7a). Pull the thread taut (7b).

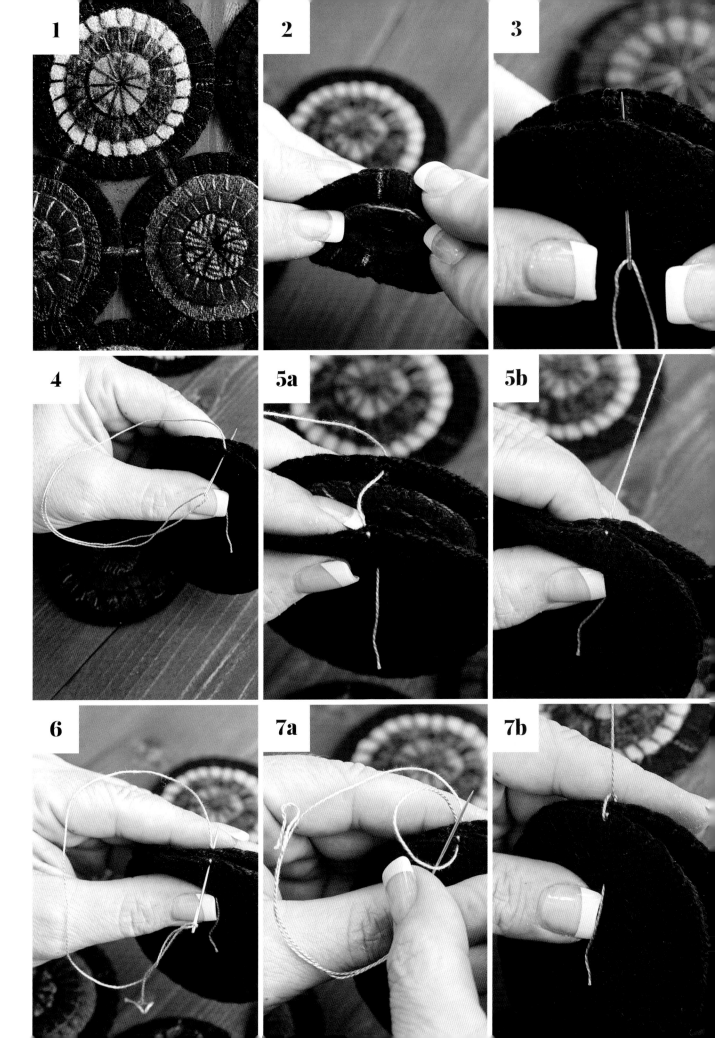

8 Circle the thread counterclockwise again, pierce the wool of the two pennies at the same spot again, and thread the tip of your needle through the loop, making a second knot to secure (8). Pull taut. Two knots is the trick to securing the pennies.

9 To bury the ending thread tail, insert the needle close to the tacking stitch, then exit between the two layers of the back penny (the one that doesn't have the starting tail), about ¾" away from the edge (9).

10 Pull the thread through the penny and leave a tail (10). Continuing in this manner, join all of the pennies with double-knotted tack stitches, working from the center of your project outward.

11 Before clipping any thread tails, steam your completed penny mat. To clip the thread tails, position your scissors parallel to the mat, pull up on the tail slightly (your scissor blades will be perpendicular to the thread tail), and snip (11). By holding the scissors this way, you won't accidentally clip your mat. Repeat to clip all of the thread tails.

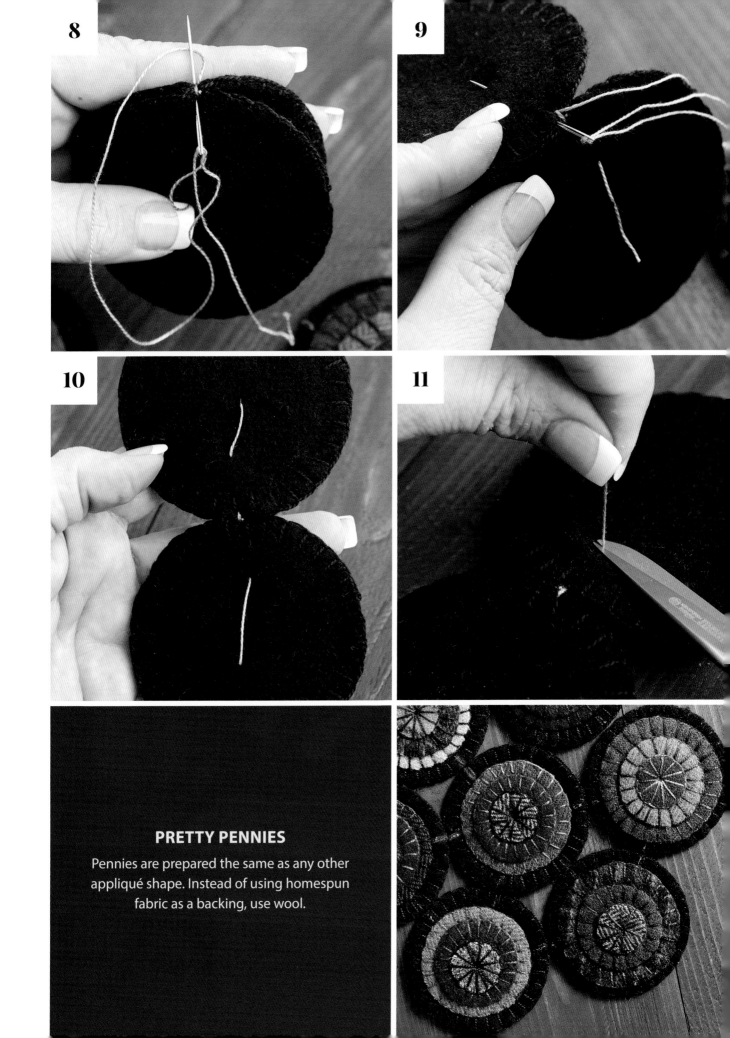

PRETTY PENNIES

Pennies are prepared the same as any other appliqué shape. Instead of using homespun fabric as a backing, use wool.

STITCHES

The stitches are the frosting on the wool cakes. Sure, they keep the appliqués permanently in place, but they also add interest and dimensional details. Use a length of thread approximately 18" long when working the stitches. Any longer than that and your thread will tangle and start to look scruffy after repeatedly pulling it through the fabric. Make sure you're working in a comfortable position with good light over the shoulder opposite your dominant hand.

Note to left-handed stitchers: The use of the terms *dominant hand* and *nondominant hand* is consistent throughout the step-by-step stitch instructions. You'll do everything the opposite of what is described in the instructions. For example, if I work on the left-hand side, you'll work on the right-hand side. The same is true of the swing of the thread—go in the opposite direction of what's written. You can do it!

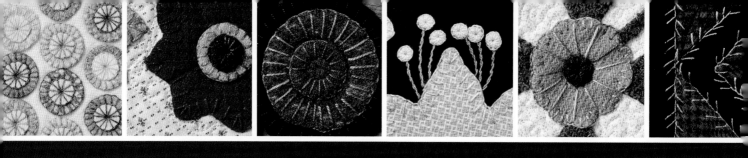

Blanket Stitch

The blanket stitch is used around the outer edge of appliqué shapes or to finish edges. It can be stitched long or short, straight or angled, spaced closely together or far apart. Its versatility is why it's my go-to stitch!

1 To make the basic stitch, bring the threaded needle up from the back of the work so it comes out right next to the top edge of the appliqué shape (1).

2 Pull the needle through to the top until the knot is against the back. As you do this, keep your middle finger pressed against the eye of the needle to prevent unthreading the needle (2).

3 Pull the thread up and away from the appliqué shape (away from the edge where you're working) with your non-sewing hand (3). Anchor the emerging thread with your thumb to keep a bit of tension on it before moving ahead.

4 Position your needle perpendicular to the appliqué edge and put the tip into the appliqué directly beneath the starting point (4). Your thread should make a counterclockwise (clockwise for lefties) loop above and to the left of your needle. See the photo; thread placement is key to completing the stitch.

5 Bring the needle tip back up to the front at the starting point, with the thread just behind the needle tip (5).

6 Pull the needle and thread through (6a). Pull the thread in the direction you want it to lie; in this case, pull the needle away from you (not toward you) and perpendicular to the shape (6b). Doing so will help your stitch stay flat and straight.

7 Before making the next stitch, sweep your non-sewing hand upward (over the stitch you just made), pulling the thread over and keeping tension on the thread at all times. (Your thread is never left unattended.) This keeps the stitch from rolling back and being misshaped. Working counterclockwise (clockwise for lefties) and holding the thread up and away as before, insert the needle one stitch length to the left (7). Bring the needle tip up in front of the thread that's wrapped counterclockwise as before.

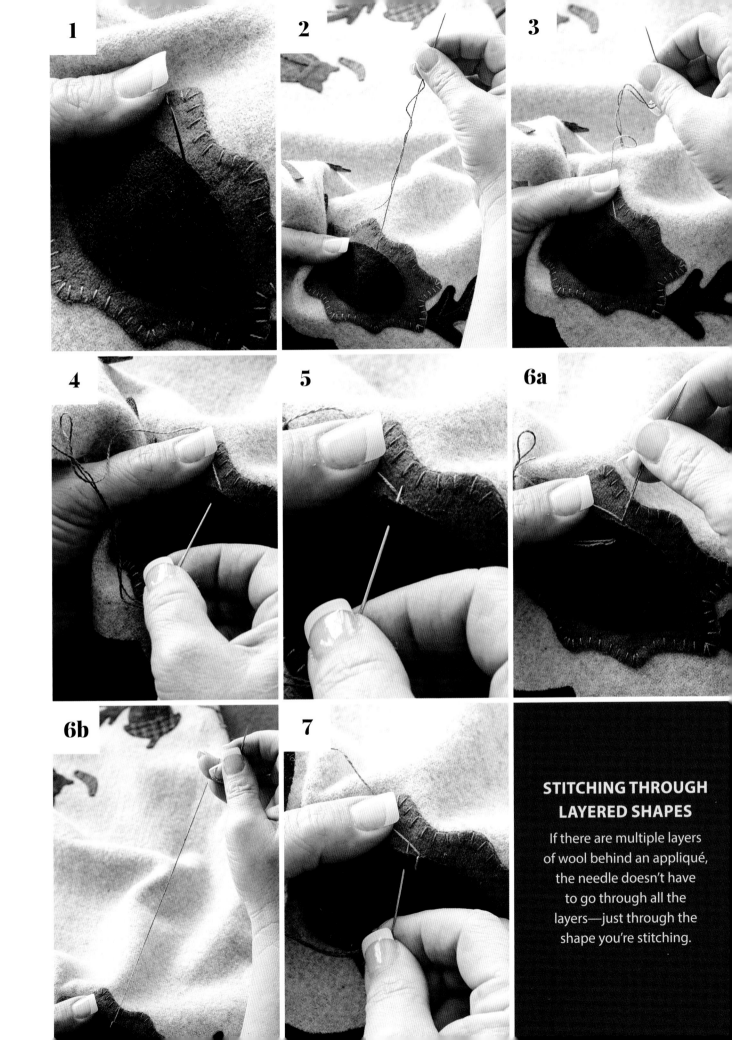

1

2

3

4

5

6a

6b

7

STITCHING THROUGH LAYERED SHAPES

If there are multiple layers of wool behind an appliqué, the needle doesn't have to go through all the layers—just through the shape you're stitching.

8 To control tension on your stitching, keep your thumb inside the thread loop as you pull the needle up and away as before (8). Note: Always check to make sure the thread is behind the needle tip before you pull the stitch through.

9 Once the thread is taut, pull your thumb out and pull the stitch taut (9) but not so tight that it sinks in and separates your wool fibers.

10 Continue working counterclockwise around the shape (10) and continue to keep tension on the thread at all times.

11 To tie off a thread when you're coming to the end or completing a shape, stop stitching when you have between 3" and 4" of thread remaining. Insert the needle tip into the background at the outside edge of the perpendicular stitch (11a). Pull the needle to the back of your work (11b and 11c).

12 On the back of the work, insert the needle close to the emerging thread and take a small bite of the background (12a). Pull the thread through, leaving a small loop (12b). Don't pull the thread taut!

13 Insert your needle through the thread loop once and pull the thread through loosely, keeping the loop intact (13).

CONTROLLING THREAD TENSION

Just like the tension on your sewing machine, you need tension on the thread when you're hand stitching in order to control the thread at all times. Use your thumb to provide that tension (see inset). This helps your stitches stay in place, and it keeps the thread from twisting, wobbling, and getting tangled. Avoid the thread acrobatics of pulling the thread toward you and rolling your arm around to position the stitch; instead, pull perpendicular and get the stitch to lie flat where you position it by keeping tension on the thread.

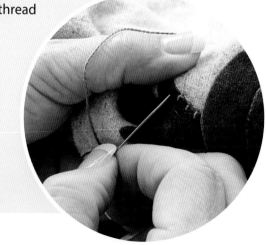

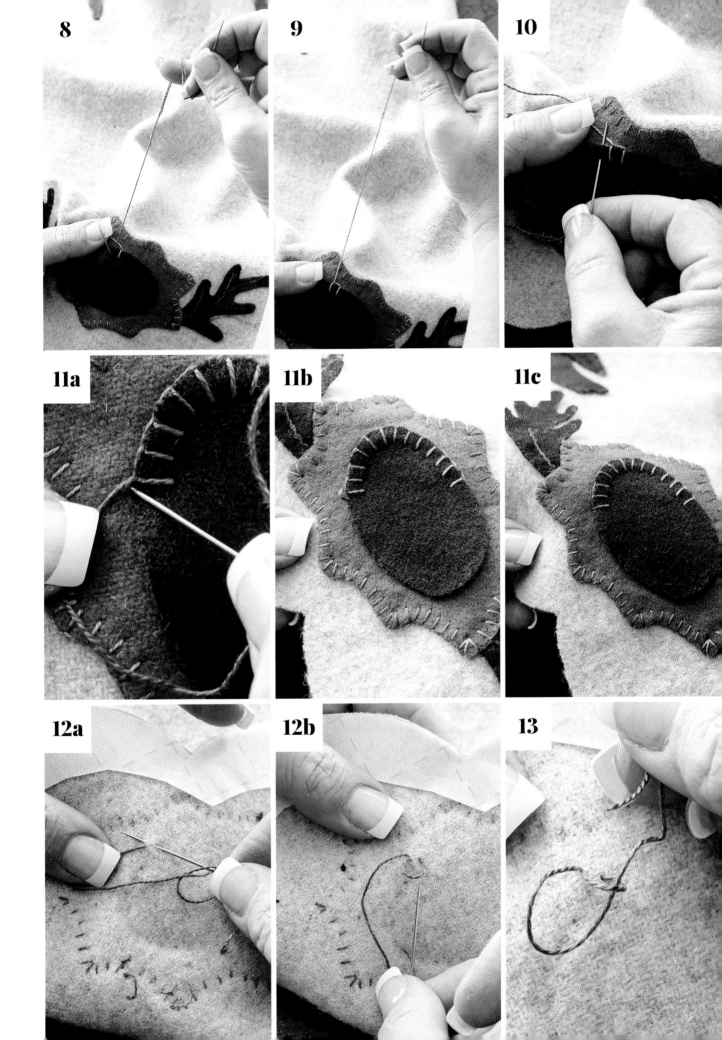

14 Go through the thread loop a second time in the same direction (14).

15 Pull the thread taut to form a surgical knot on the back of your work (15).

16 The surgical knot should securely sink down into the background next to the wool; clip the thread end (16).

17 To begin a new thread and continue stitching, bring the needle up from behind the appliqué, inserting the needle tip at the outside edge of the previous stitch, between the appliqué shape and the thread that covers the edge (17).

18 Pull the thread through to the top until the knot is against the back and turn the thread counterclockwise, up and out of the way as before. Then insert the needle into the appliqué shape one stitch length away as before (18).

19 With the working thread behind the needle tip, pull the needle through to complete the stitch (19a). Continue as before (19b).

20 To end your stitching after stitching around an entire shape, insert the needle in the 90° corner at the outer edge of the appliqué where the first stitch was made. Tie off the thread on the back with a surgical knot as before (20).

WORK FROM THE OUTSIDE IN

When stitching circles or stacked "pennies," always begin stitching at the outside edge of the circle.

If you draw an inside circle on the penny and stitch to that line (below left), the result is often more pleasing than if you just eyeball it as you stitch (below right). When stitching around circles, the stitches get closer together at the center and are farther apart around the outside.

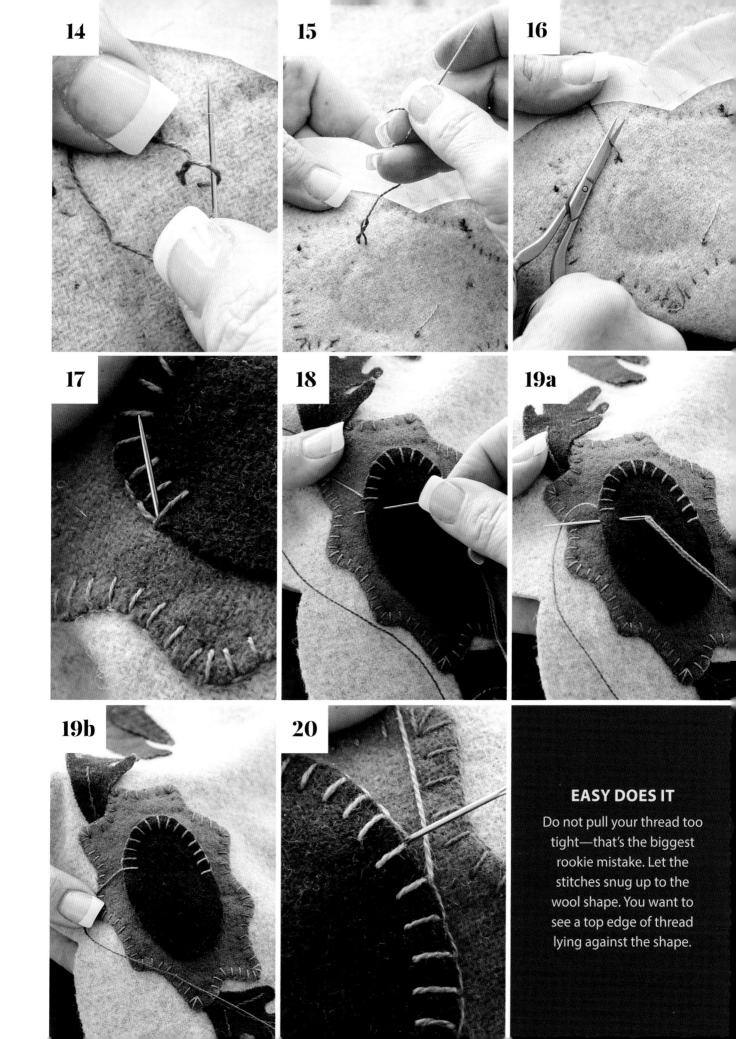

14

15

16

17

18

19a

19b

20

EASY DOES IT

Do not pull your thread too tight—that's the biggest rookie mistake. Let the stitches snug up to the wool shape. You want to see a top edge of thread lying against the shape.

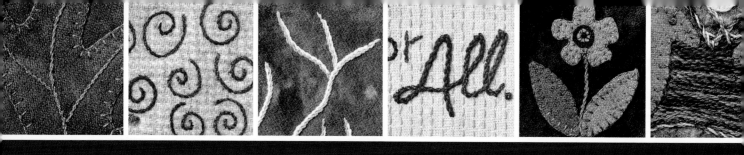

Stem Stitch

Stem stitches create details like flower stems, leaf veins, and basket handles. This stitch is also a great choice for lettering. For best results, mark the line to be stitched on the fabric before beginning.

1 Insert the threaded needle from the back of the fabric at the beginning of the drawn line (1). Bring the needle to the top, pulling the thread through until the knot is against the back.

2 Move the thread in a counterclockwise circle up and away from the line, holding tension on the thread with your nondominant thumb (2).

3 Insert the needle ⅛" away from the emerging thread and bring the tip up in the same hole as the previous stitch (3), keeping the thread below the needle as you pull it through. It's very important that the thread always be thrown in the counterclockwise direction, even if you're left handed. Throwing counterclockwise makes the finished stitches appear more like a twisted rope; throwing the thread in the opposite direction results in a tighter, wirelike twist.

4 Pull the needle through, keeping tension on the thread with your thumb (4a). Avoid pulling the stitch too tight. The thread should rest gently atop the wool, not sink into your appliqué shape. After completing the stitch, circle the thread counterclockwise behind your thumb and prepare to make another stitch (4b).

PULL BACK

Using your thumb to hold the thread tension, pull back slightly on your thread to open up the previous stem stitch's opening where you'll insert the needle to make your next stitch.

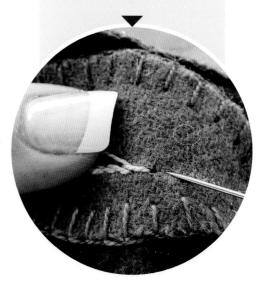

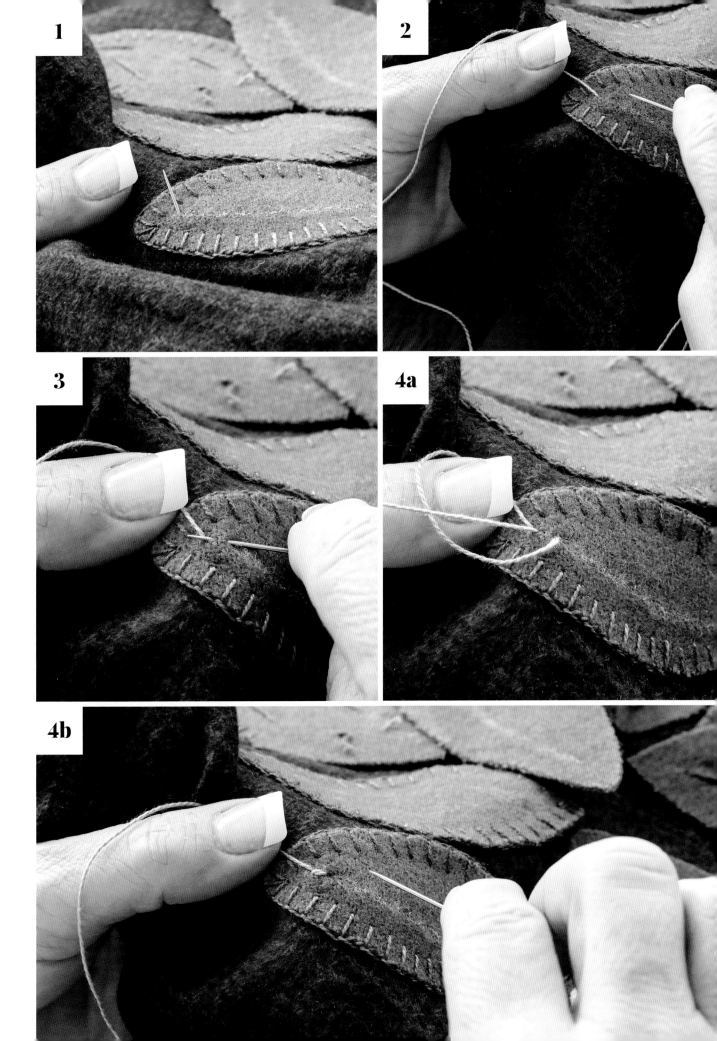

5 Insert the needle ⅛" away from the previous stitch (5a) and bring the tip up in the same hole as the previous stitch. Pull the needle through as before to complete a second stitch (5b).

6 Continue in the same manner to reach the end of the stem-stitch line (6).

7 To finish the line of stitching, insert the needle about ¹⁄₁₆" forward from the final stitch (7a), and pull the thread and needle to the back (7b). Knot your thread on the back of your work (see page 46).

SUBSTANTIAL STEMS

If you want more substantial lines than a single stem stitch creates (top), consider stitching two rows side by side (middle). For an even thicker line, place three rows side by side (bottom).

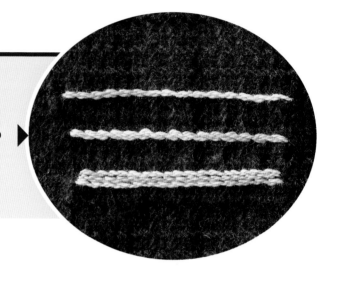

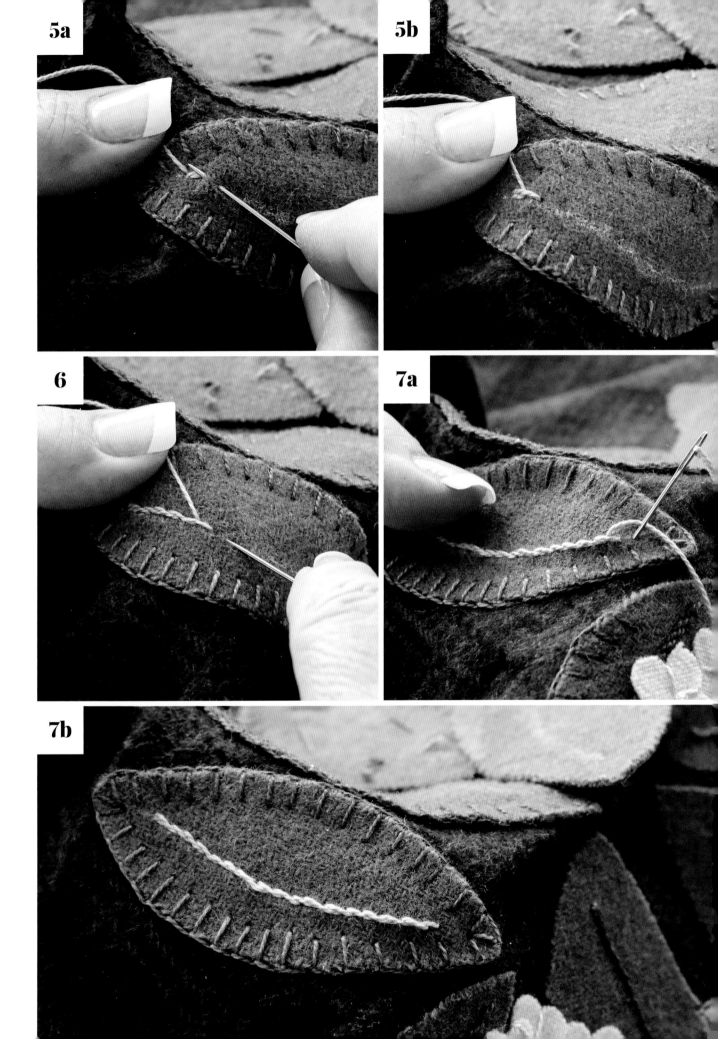

Cross-Stitch

I most often use cross-stitches to secure stems, vines, and basket handles to the background. Rather than straight stitching up one side and down the other on skinny appliqué strips, I cross-stitch them. It adds a different texture and secures the appliqué at the same time. Follow along for my tips to get the look I love!

1 Hold your work with the stem running horizontally (rather than vertically.) Bring up the needle from the back of your work in the background at the top corner of the appliqué strip (1). Pull the needle and thread all the way through until the knot is against the back.

2 Cross the thread over the appliqué to show half of the X. Insert the tip of the needle into the background only (not into the appliqué) at the lower edge of the appliqué stem where the base of the X thread will lie, about ¼" to the left of where the first stitch emerged (2). Bring the needle tip out perpendicular to the stem, exactly above the position where your needle went into the background. This is the only time you will need to lay the thread across the stem.

3 Pull the thread through but not too taut (3). You want your thread to rest gently on the stem and not sink into the wool.

4 Position the thread in a clockwise fashion above and away from where it emerged. Insert the needle in the background below the stem and ¼" away from the last stitch (4); bring the tip out just above the stem. Keep the needle perpendicular to the stem.

5 Hereafter, use the thread emerging at the top of the stem as a guide for determining the distance between stitches (5). The needle tip should come out ¼" to the left of the thread and be perpendicular to the stem. The half X will form as the needle is pulled through.

6 Continue in the same manner to make half-X stitches the entire length of the appliqué (6). At the end of the appliqué, your needle and thread should emerge at the top corner of the appliqué strip.

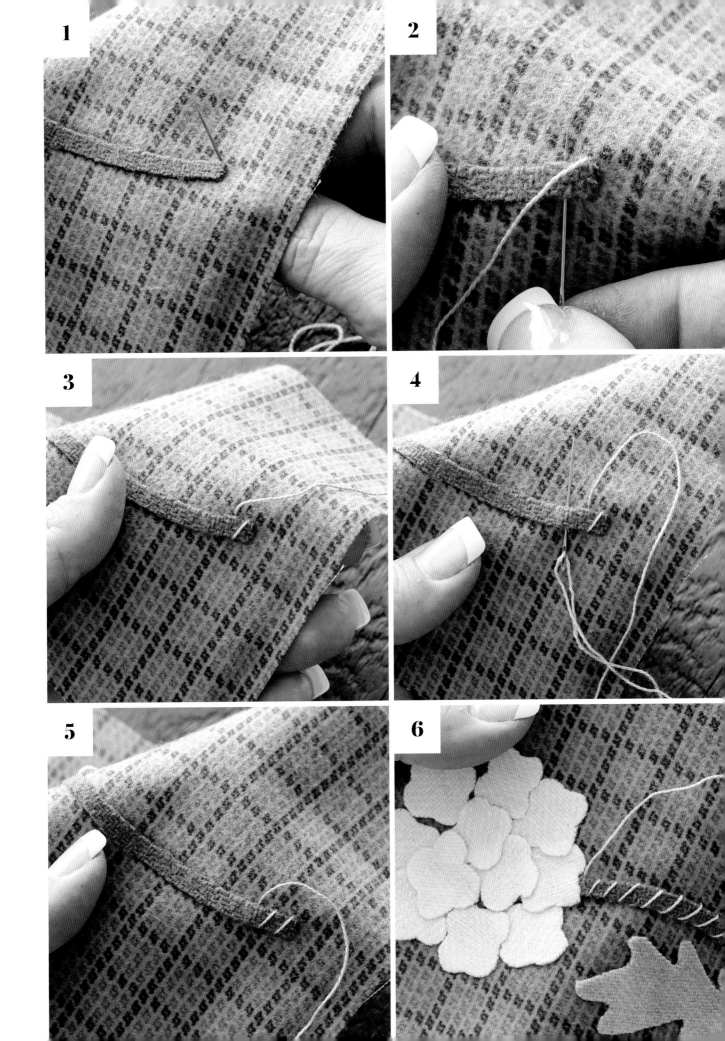

7 Now, swing the emerging thread counterclockwise and position it to cross over the first half X (7a). Insert your needle tip into the background below the appliqué at the base of the second half X and come up above the appliqué in the background at the top of the first half X to complete a full X (7b).

8 To continue, position the thread counterclockwise again and insert the needle below the stem in the background at the base of the third half X. Bring up the needle at the top of the second half X (8).

9 Pull the needle through the stitch completely but not too taut, remembering to gently rest the thread on the wool (9).

10 Continue to stitch the entire stem with cross-stitches (10). At the completion of the last X, knot the thread on the back of your work (see page 46).

VARY THE SIZE

Cross-stiches can vary in size depending on the width of the appliqué strip you are stitching over. Experiment with spacing your stitches farther apart or closer together to get the look you're after. You may also want to try working cross-stitches over a line of stem stitches to add more dimension (inset). The choice is up to you!

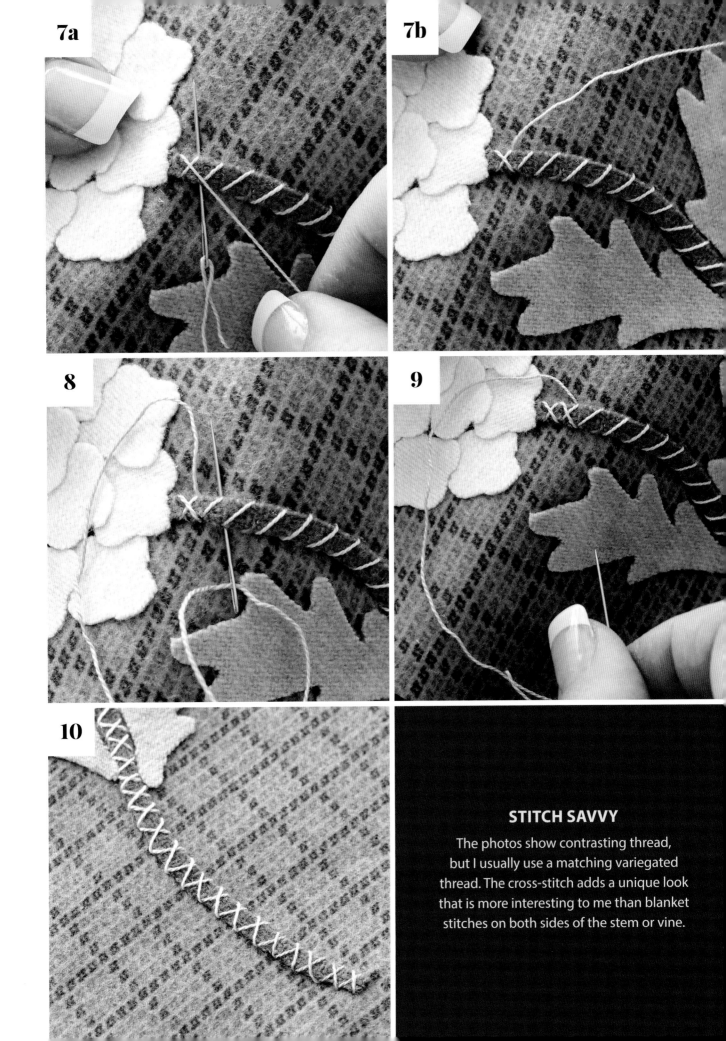

7a

7b

8

9

10

STITCH SAVVY

The photos show contrasting thread, but I usually use a matching variegated thread. The cross-stitch adds a unique look that is more interesting to me than blanket stitches on both sides of the stem or vine.

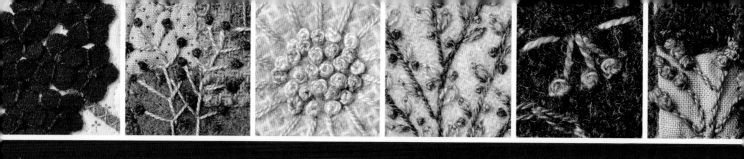

Colonial Knots

To make colonial knots, I always work on a pillow positioned on my lap. The pillow helps hold the needle while I'm pulling on the working thread, so I get a nice, tight knot and not a loose, wobbly mess. As a rule, colonial knots don't flop over like French knots sometimes do. That's why this is my go-to knot!

1 Bring the threaded needle from the back of the work to the right side through the appliqué at the point where you want the finished knot (1). Pull the thread through until the knot is against the back.

2 Holding the thread in your left hand with some slack and the needle in your right hand, position the needle on top of and perpendicular to the emerging thread (2).

3 Slide the needle tip to the right and underneath the thread (3).

4 Rotate the needle tip counterclockwise to form a loop around the needle (4).

5 With your left hand going over the tip of the needle, loop the working thread around the needle three times (5).

6 With tension on the working thread pulling the loops taut, slide the thread loops toward the center of the needle (6).

LETTING GO

Notice that when I'm making colonial knots I am *not* holding on to my project. The project nests on the pillow in my lap while I work the knot.

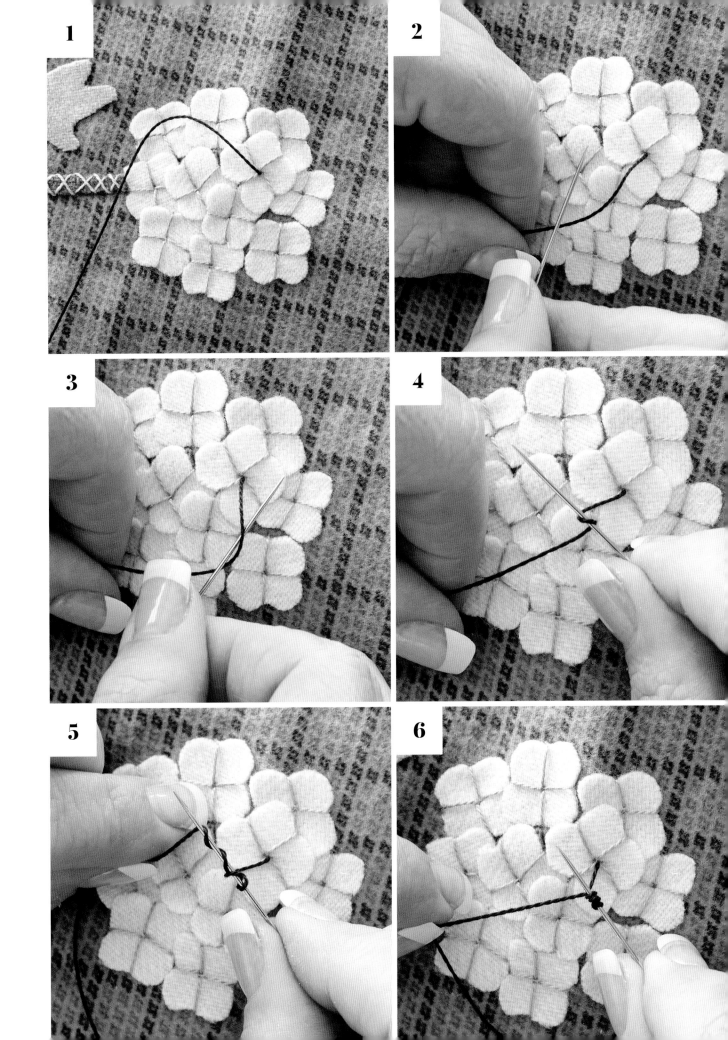

7 Keeping the thread loops on the needle, position the needle tip down and into the appliqué at the finished knot point, stabbing it partway into the pillow in your lap so that the needle eye is upright (7). Maintain tension on the working thread, pulling it taut as you slide the needle into the appliqué. This enables you to pull on the thread to create a nice, tight knot.

8 Using your left thumb to keep the tension on the thread (8a), move your right hand to the underside of your work to pull the needle out of the pillow and through the appliqué to the back of your work, completing the knot (8b).

KNOT SIZE

Knot size can be achieved in two ways: by changing the number of thread wraps around the needle or by changing the thread weight/size (below, clockwise from top knot).

- Single strand of thread + 3 wraps = standard-size knot

- Single strand of thread + 1 wrap = tiny knot

- Double strand of thread + 3 wraps = large knot

- Double strand of thread + 1 wrap = standard-size knot with less "work" wrapping. Use this method when you have lots and lots of knots and want to stitch faster. Work smarter, not harder!

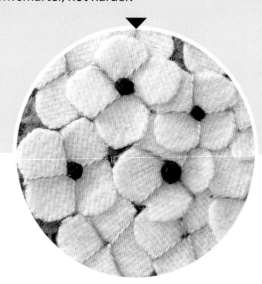

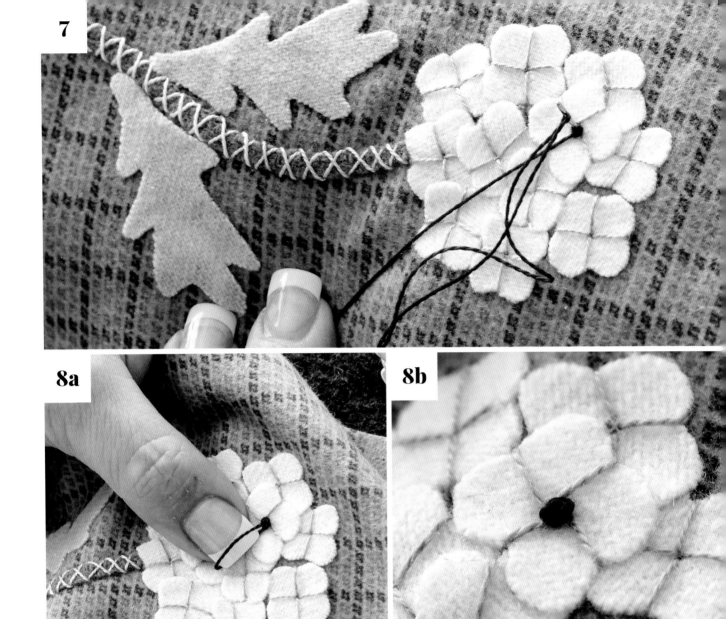

7

8a

8b

STITCHING POSTURE

Do you ever have back and neck pain while you're stitching or after you've stitched for a while? Poor posture is usually the culprit, but there's a way to avoid hunching over your work and the pain that goes with it. I place a travel-sized pillow on my lap and use it as a surface for my work. The pillow helps me sit back in the chair, which makes me sit up straight and ultimately leads to better stitching.

Featherstitch

When you're working the featherstitch, you're making U shapes. Imagine a centerline—one of the U shapes always straddles this line. The next U is either completely to the left or completely to the right but still touching the shoulder of the previous U before or after it. As my friend Sally says, the easiest way to remember where to place each stitch is "shoulder, shoulder, belly." Here we go!

1 In these photos, the edge of the white wool represents the centerline (belly) of the featherstitch. Bring the threaded needle from the back of your work to the front, with the needle coming through the appliqué ⅛" from the centerline (left shoulder) of the stitch (1). Pull the thread through to the front until the knot is against the back.

2 Hold the emerging thread with your left thumb to keep it taut (2).

3 Insert the point of the needle ⅛" to the right of the centerline and just across from the first stitch (left shoulder and right shoulder). Bring the needle up just to the right of the centerline (belly) and ¼" below the shoulders (3).

4 Pull the needle through, keeping the needle above the thread loop to form the U (4).

5 Pull the thread taut and keep tension on the trailing thread with your left thumb (5), remembering to gently rest the thread on the wool and not pull it too tight.

6 Where your thread emerged is the new left shoulder of the next U. Swing the thread below to form a U and insert the needle at the right shoulder of the U; bring the needle back up at the belly, centered beneath this new U (not on the centerline). The spacing should be approximately ¼" from side to side and top to bottom (6).

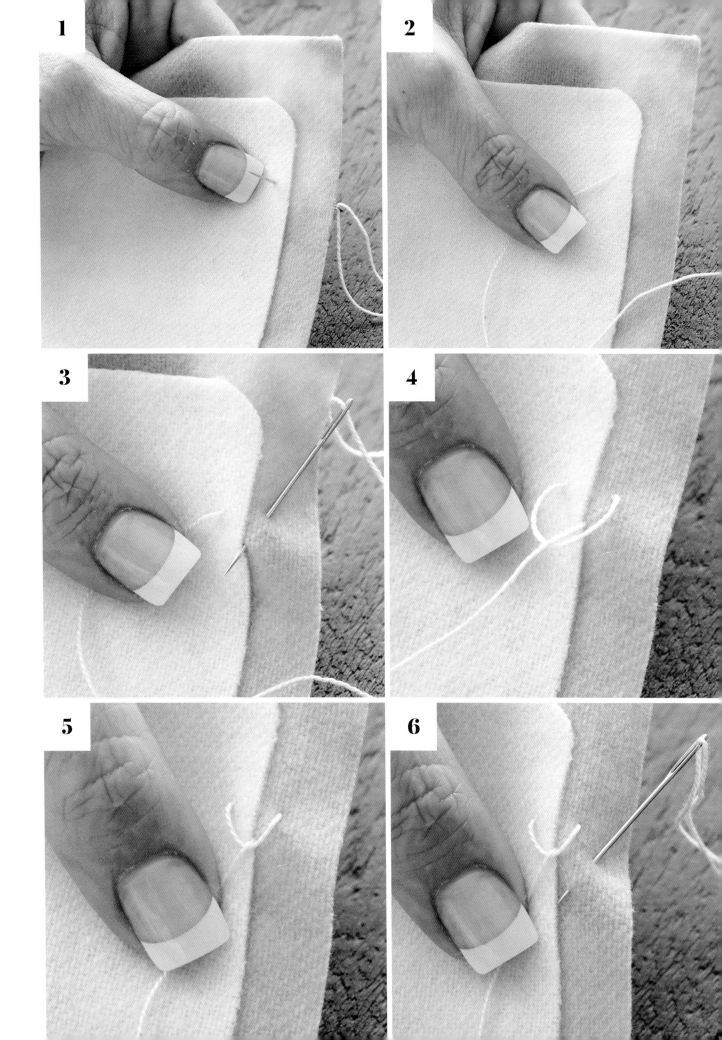

7 Pull the stitch through, keeping the needle above the thread loop to make a U. Keep the tension on the trailing thread with your left thumb (7).

8 The next U will be aligned along the centerline again. The emerging thread is the right shoulder of this U. Swing your thread down into a U shape and insert the needle in the left shoulder of the U with the tip emerging ¼" down on the centerline (8). Yes, this is a bit awkward.

9 Keep the needle above the thread loop as you pull the thread through, completing the third U (9).

10 Repeat to continue adding U shapes, alternating between the centerline and just to the right of the centerline (10).

11 To end a row of stitching, always stop at the bottom (belly) of a U. Insert your needle to the wrong side, crossing over the thread just next to where your needle emerged (11a); proceed to make your ending knot on the back (see page 46). You're featherstitching!

12 To start again, the thread emerges at the inside base of the U (see blue dot on 11b). You'll cross over the thread at the base of the U in making your next stitch.

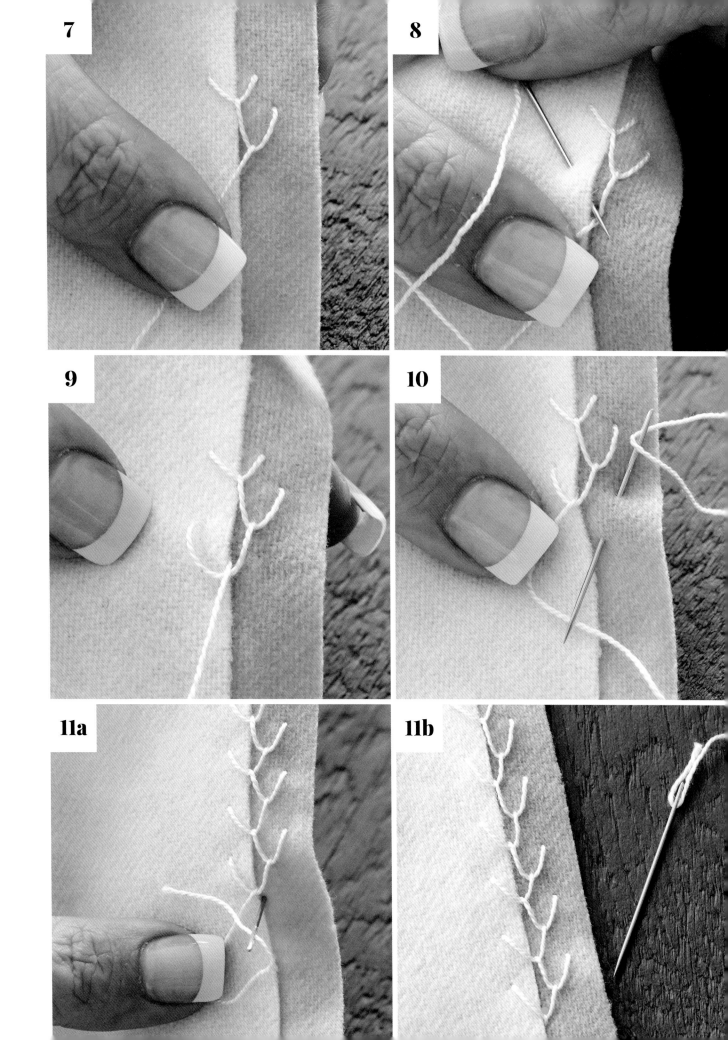

Fly Stitch

The fly stitch is similar to the featherstitch, but it is usually worked either as a single stitch or in straight rows following a marked centerline. Vary the length and width of fly stitches to add to its versatility.

1 Bring your needle up from the back of the work and emerge at the top of the drawn line. (The line will be the centerline of your fly stitch.) Pull the thread through until the knot is against the back. Position your thread in a counterclockwise C, with your thumb holding tension on the emerging thread (1).

2 Working down the marked centerline, insert your needle on the drawn line approximately ¼" below where the thread emerged (2).

3 Without pulling the stitch through entirely, bring the needle tip out through the appliqué and under the thread at a 45° angle to the line (3). The distance from where the needle was inserted and where it came out will be the length of the stitch, in this instance ⅛" to ³⁄₁₆" away from the outer edge of the appliqué.

4 Pull the needle through (4). Stitches where the needle emerges to the left of the drawn line will always form the spine of the fly stitch.

5 Using your left thumb to keep tension on the working thread, position the thread loop in a U beneath the drawn line, and swing your needle to the opposite side. Insert the needle tip on the right side of the spine directly across and an equal distance from the edge of the appliqué as the first stitch. Bring the tip of the needle up through the same hole as the bottom of the last stitch of the spine (5).

6 Pull the needle through, with the needle tip going over the working thread to create the Y in the fly stitch (6).

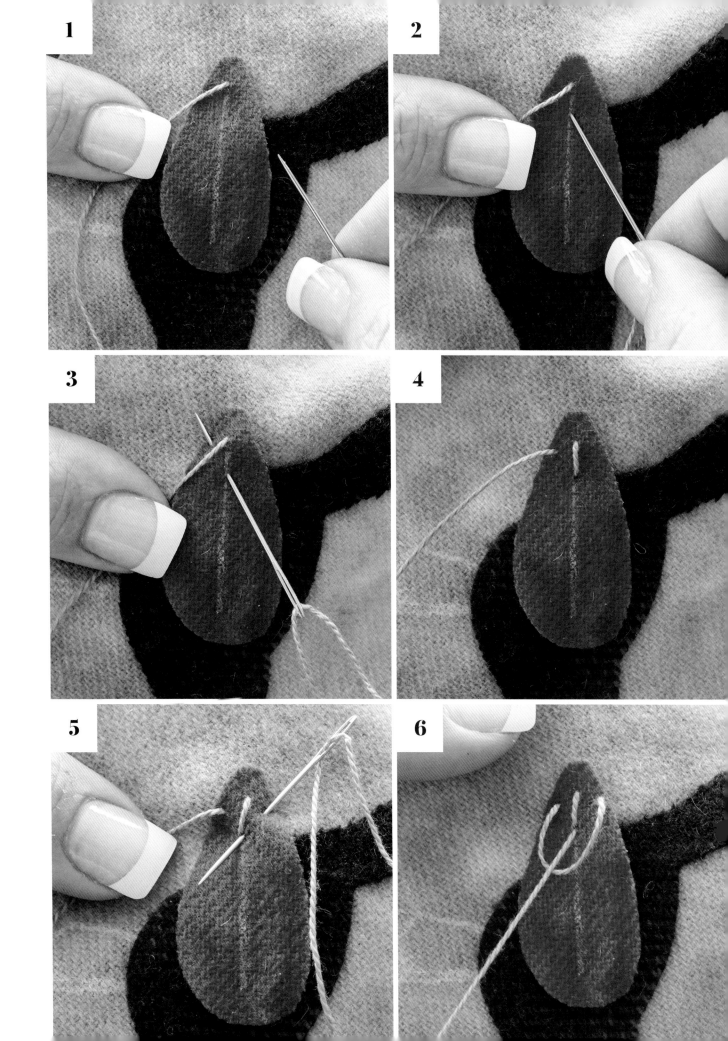

7 Holding the emerging thread taut with your thumb (7a), again insert the needle tip ¼" down from where the thread came out on the marked line and bring it out at a 45° angle to the line (7b). The stitch should be the same distance from the appliqué outer edge as the other stitches. On a leaf shape, this means your stitch length will get longer as the leaf widens.

8 Pull the needle through to create the next section of the spine (8).

9 Again, position the thread loop in a U beneath the drawn line and swing your needle to the opposite side. Insert the needle tip on the right side of the spine directly across and an equal distance from the edge of the appliqué. Bring the tip of the needle up through the same hole as the bottom of the last stitch of the spine (9).

10 Continue stitching until you've reached the end of your drawn line, finishing the row of fly stitches by pulling the threaded needle to the back of your work near the same hole you emerged (10). You're fly stitching!

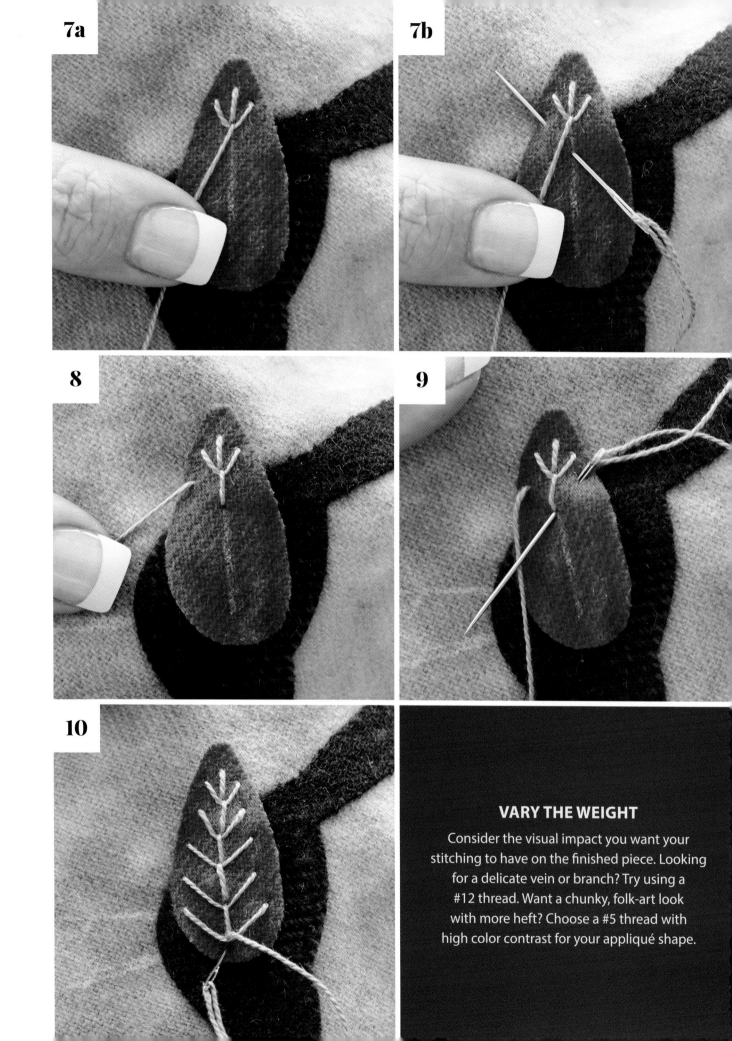

7a

7b

8

9

10

VARY THE WEIGHT

Consider the visual impact you want your stitching to have on the finished piece. Looking for a delicate vein or branch? Try using a #12 thread. Want a chunky, folk-art look with more heft? Choose a #5 thread with high color contrast for your appliqué shape.

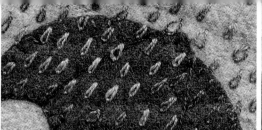

Lazy Daisy Stitch

As the name implies, this stitch most often resembles a daisy petal, but it could be buds, leaves, or even raindrops. It's normally used as an embellishment and not to hold an appliqué in place.

1 Bring the threaded needle from the back of the work to the front and pull the thread through until the knot is against the back. Holding the thread with your left thumb for tension, swing the working thread clockwise (1).

2 Insert the needle tip right next to the hole where the thread emerged. Bring the needle back up at the spot where you want the top of the first petal to be, keeping the needle tip over the thread loop (2).

3 Pull the needle through to create the first petal (3), remembering to gently rest the thread on the wool and not pull it too tight.

4 Pull the stitch taut, making sure to leave the petal open (4a). If you pull too tight, the petal will close. To secure the petal, insert the needle tip just on the other side of the thread forming the petal loop and close to where the thread came out (4b). One lazy daisy stitch is complete.

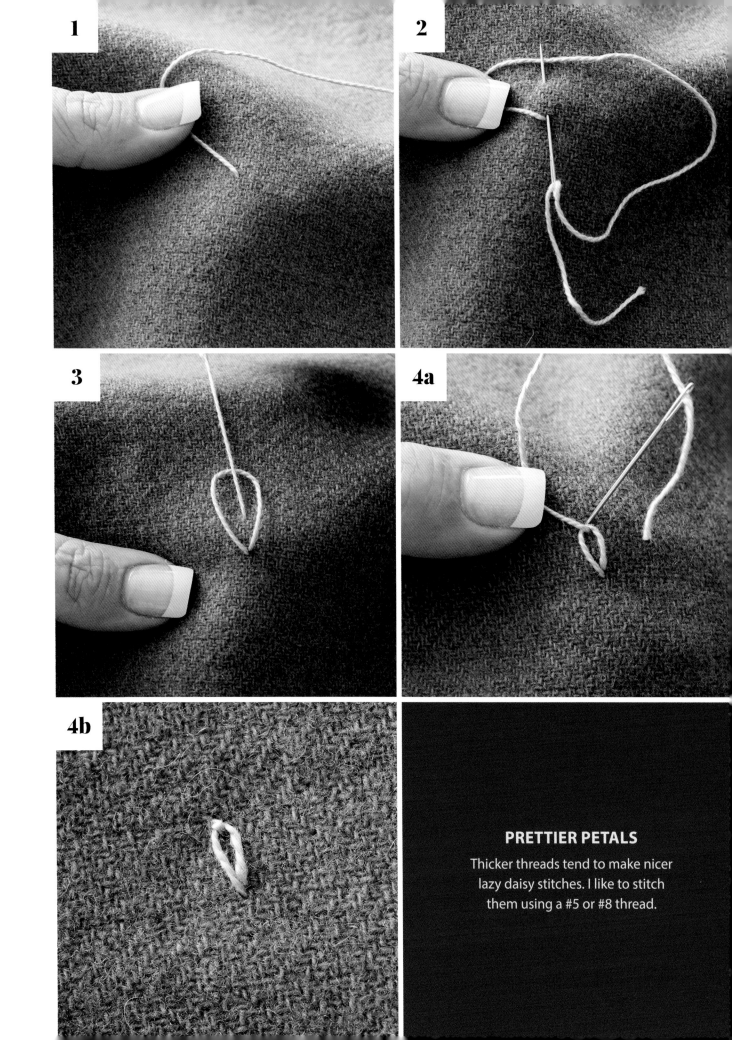

1

2

3

4a

4b

PRETTIER PETALS

Thicker threads tend to make nicer lazy daisy stitches. I like to stitch them using a #5 or #8 thread.

5 To make a full daisy, I suggest working the petals in a north, south, west, east order. Bring the needle up again at the center. Insert the needle back into the center and bring the needle back out at the top of the second petal (5a). Pull the stitch taut, making sure to leave the petal open, and insert the needle tip to the opposite side of the petal loop to secure the tip of and complete the second lazy daisy petal. Bring the needle up again from behind the center (5b).

6 For the third petal (on the west side), insert the needle back into the center and bring the needle back out at the top of the third petal (6a) and repeat as before to complete the third lazy daisy petal (6b.)

7 Repeat to make the fourth petal on the east side (7a, 7b).

8 Once you've completed the "east" petal, make four additional lazy daisy petals, one between each of the first four petals, for an eight-petal flower (8). Making them in this manner ensures more symmetrical flowers, as opposed to going around in a circle and squeezing petals too close or too far apart at the end.

9 Your flower always looks a little wonky at this point until you put a colonial knot (page 58) in the center to cover where all the stitches come together (9).

LAZY DAISY LEAVES

To make leaves, zigzag lazy daisy stitches down alternate sides of a stem stitch stem (page 50). Choose threads to match your flower (inset) or use green thread for a more literal translation.

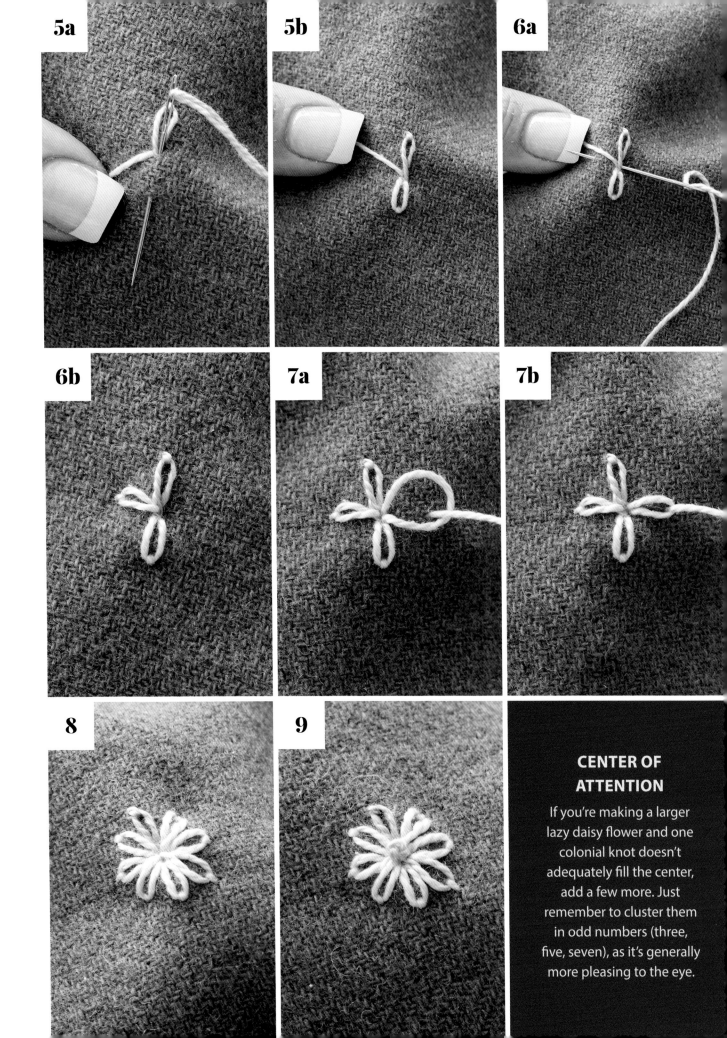

5a

5b

6a

6b

7a

7b

8

9

CENTER OF ATTENTION

If you're making a larger lazy daisy flower and one colonial knot doesn't adequately fill the center, add a few more. Just remember to cluster them in odd numbers (three, five, seven), as it's generally more pleasing to the eye.

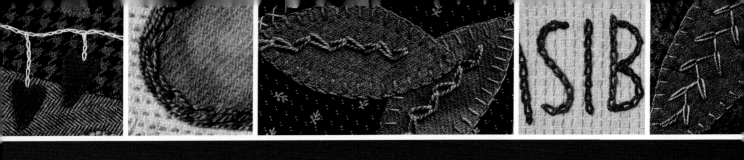

Chain Stitch

The chain stitch is great for stitching words or letters. It's a variation of the lazy daisy stitch, but it forms a continuous line rather than a single petal. That makes chain stitching go a little more quickly, which I always appreciate!

1 Bring the threaded needle from the back of the work through to the front and pull the thread through until the knot is against the back. Holding the thread with the left thumb for tension, swing the working thread clockwise (1).

2 Insert the needle tip right into the hole where the thread emerged. Because you're sticking the needle back into the same hole where the knot is, hold the knot underneath the fabric to one side out of the way so you don't pierce it. Bring the needle back up at the spot where you want the top of the first chain stitch to be, keeping the needle on top of the thread loop (2).

3 Pull the needle through, creating the first chain (3). Pull the stitch taut, making sure to leave the chain open. (If you pull too tight, the chain will close.)

4 Insert the needle tip inside the chain loop close to the top where the thread is already emerging. Keep the working thread swinging clockwise above the chain to create the next loop. The tip of the needle should come back up at the top of the second chain loop (4a), making sure the needle crosses over the top of the loop to form a second chain. Pull the needle through to complete a second loop in the chain (4b).

5 Continue in the same manner, always going back into the chain loop next to where the thread emerges and coming out at the top of the next chain loop (5), remembering not to pull too tight.

6 To end a row of chain stitching, go over the last chain loop rather than next to the emerging thread with your final stitch (6a) to secure the last loop (like making a lazy daisy stitch; see page 70). Knot the thread on the back of your finished row (6b).

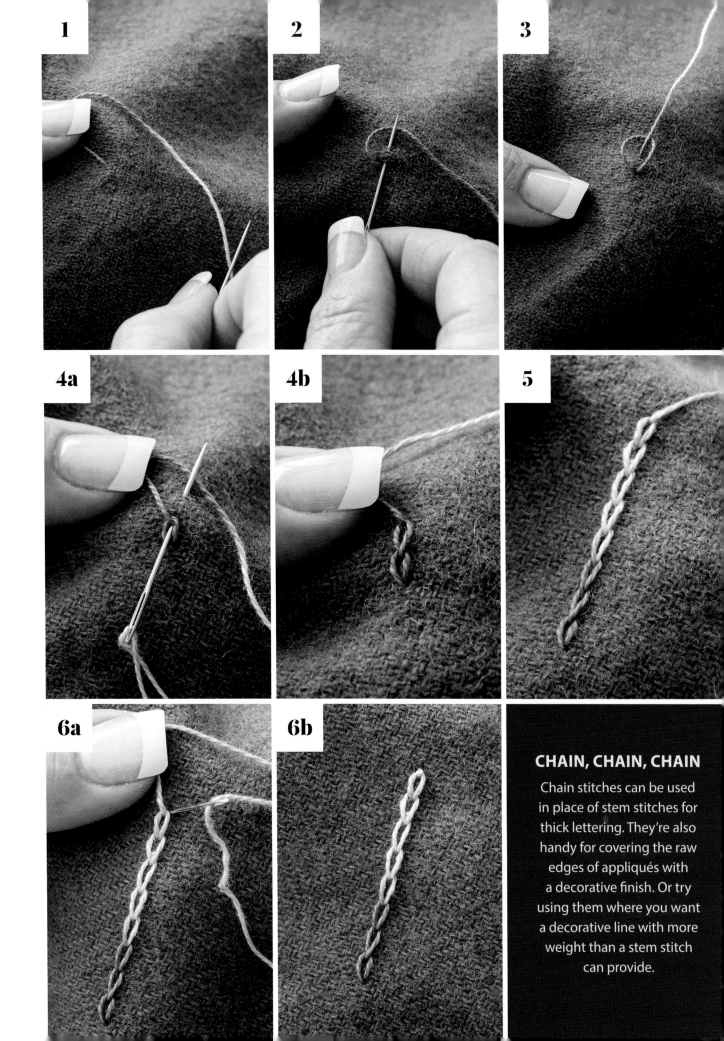

1

2

3

4a

4b

5

6a

6b

CHAIN, CHAIN, CHAIN

Chain stitches can be used in place of stem stitches for thick lettering. They're also handy for covering the raw edges of appliqués with a decorative finish. Or try using them where you want a decorative line with more weight than a stem stitch can provide.

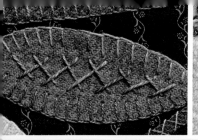

Herringbone Stitch

A lot of times I work this stitch on herringbone wool, because the wool pattern gives me a horizontal line to follow. If you need to, use a liquid chalk marker to draw two horizontal lines parallel to each other, and follow those until you get the hang of this stitch.

1 Bring your threaded needle up from the back of your work at the end of the top line and pull the thread until the knot is against the back. Pull the working thread across the wool and down to the lower line to form a half X. Insert the needle tip into the line at the point where the diagonal thread crosses it (do not go through the thread) and bring it out on the line a generous ¼" to the left (1).

2 Pull the thread taut to complete one half of the first herringbone (2).

3 Bring the working thread across the diagonal stitch and insert the needle on the line at the point where the top of the herringbone is completed; bring the needle back out a generous ¼" to the left of that point (3).

4 Pull the thread taut to complete the first herringbone (4). Notice that where the thread emerges on the top line is directly above where it emerges at the base of the first half of the stitch.

5 Again, position the working thread to make the first half of the second herringbone. Pull the working thread across the wool and down to the lower line. Insert the needle tip at the base of the X on the bottom line and bring it back up on the bottom line at least a generous ¼" to the left of the point where the needle went in and directly beneath where the outer thread emerges on the top line (5).

6 Pull the thread taut. Position the working thread to complete the second herringbone by pulling it up to the top line (6).

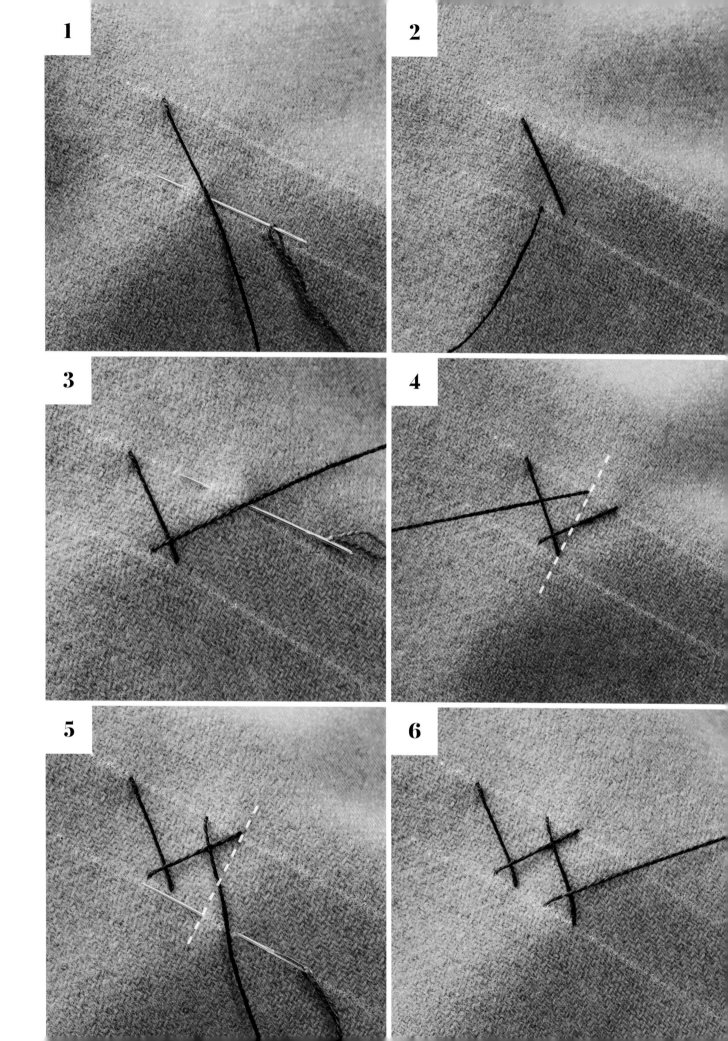

7 Insert the needle on the line at the point where the top of the herringbone is complete and bring it back out a generous ¼" to the left of that point (7). Again note that where the thread emerges on the top line is directly above where it emerges on the base of the second herringbone.

8 Pull the thread taut to complete the second herringbone (8).

9 Continue making herringbone stitches to complete your line (9). If you start on the top, end on the top by inserting your needle when the last stitch is complete. Pull the needle to the back of the work and knot it off (see page 46).

10 To make a double herringbone stitch, you'll mirror image the second row. Begin by bringing your threaded needle to the top on the bottom line, directly below where the first herringbone stitch began (10).

11 Looking at the bottom row where the threads cross to form the X, center your next bite of wool on the top line equidistant from the bottom line (11). This will never be perfect! Do your best to center it, but don't obsess over it.

12 Pull your working thread across and down to the bottom line to complete this herringbone (12).

13 Again, center your bite into the fabric below the crossed thread on the top line to complete the first herringbone of this sequence (13).

14 Continue in the same manner, always centering the bite of wool (on the top and bottom lines) in the open spaces of each herringbone stitch (14). When your stitching is complete, steam out your marked lines.

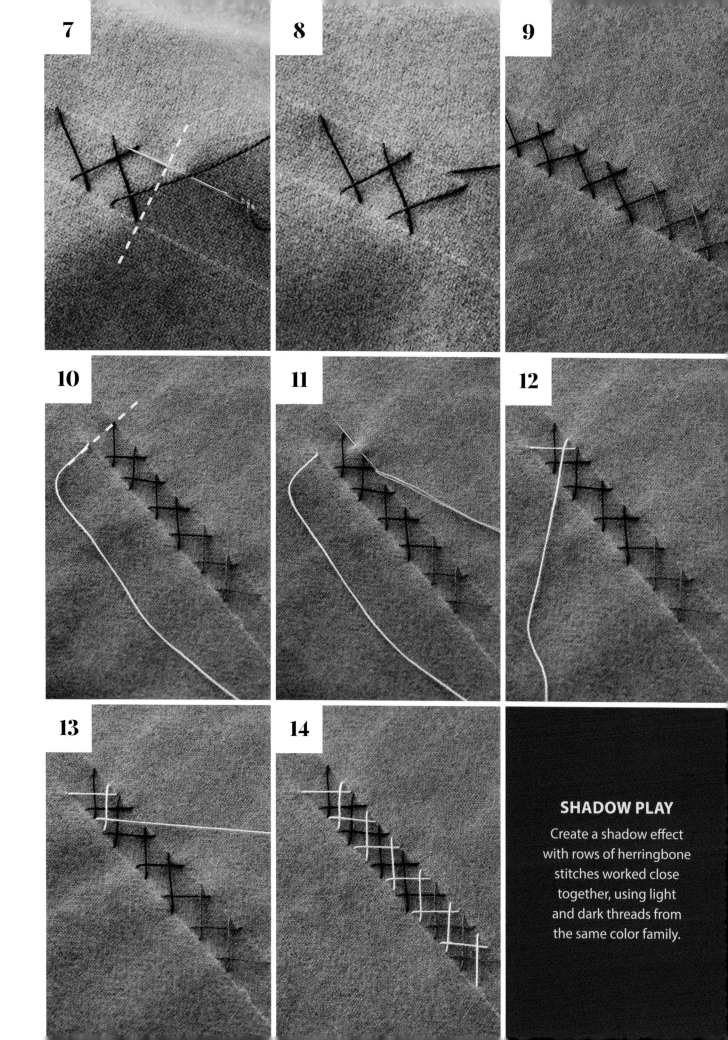

SHADOW PLAY

Create a shadow effect
with rows of herringbone
stitches worked close
together, using light
and dark threads from
the same color family.

Straight Stitch

The straight stitch is easy to work, but it can be used to create intricate details in your projects. It's simply a long, straight stitch. On its own, it can be used to make a single stem. Work several to make a cluster of flower stems or to add details to a letter. I often use it to define the petals of a one-piece flower appliqué, which is shown in the following steps. Adding some simple straight stitches secures the appliqué while allowing the petals to remain dimensional.

1 Bring up the threaded needle from the back of the work to the front at the center of an indent along the outer edge of a flower until the knot is at the back. Insert the needle tip at the flower center. Use your thumb to keep tension on the thread. Do not pull the stitch through (1).

2 Working counterclockwise, aim the needle toward the next petal and bring the needle tip up at the indentation, keeping the working thread above the needle (2a). Pull the stitch through (2b). I never stab these stitches; I always keep my needle on top of my work so I can see it. I'm constantly looking to where I'm going next, rather than going down, pulling thread through, coming up, and pulling thread through.

3 Insert the needle tip into the same hole at the flower center and come up at the next counterclockwise indentation on the flower appliqué, again keeping the thread above the needle so it isn't caught in the stitch (3). Do not pull the stitch through.

4 Come up at the next counterclockwise indentation and continue in the same manner to complete the straight stitches, rotating the project as needed to be comfortable (4).

5 To complete one flower and move to the next, insert the needle into the flower center (5a), and travel to come out with the needle at the indent of an adjacent flower (5b). Continue in this manner to stitch the remaining flowers (5c).

Drizzle Stitch

This stitch requires you to thread and unthread the needle while you're making it.
I always have my stitching pillow in my lap so that I can park the needle as I make
my stitches. I also like using two strands of thread to make the drizzle stitches
heartier. In the photos shown, I'm using one strand each of #12 and #8 thread.
Use an embellishing needle when working this stitch.

1 Bring the threaded needle from the back of the work through to the front and pull the threads until the knot is against the back (1).

2 Unthread the needle. Park the needle upright in your appliqué near where the threads emerge (2).

3 Holding the working threads with your nondominant hand, wrap the threads around the needle following these steps: position the threads in the crook of your index finger on your dominant hand, a few inches from the base of where the threads emerge (3).

4 Curl your finger (4a) and rotate it counterclockwise to make a thread loop around your finger (4b).

5 Slide the thread loop off your finger and onto the parked needle. Do not remove the needle from its position (5).

6 Leaving the loop on the needle (6a), gently pull the working threads to tighten (6b).

7 Slide the loop to the base of the parked needle (7).

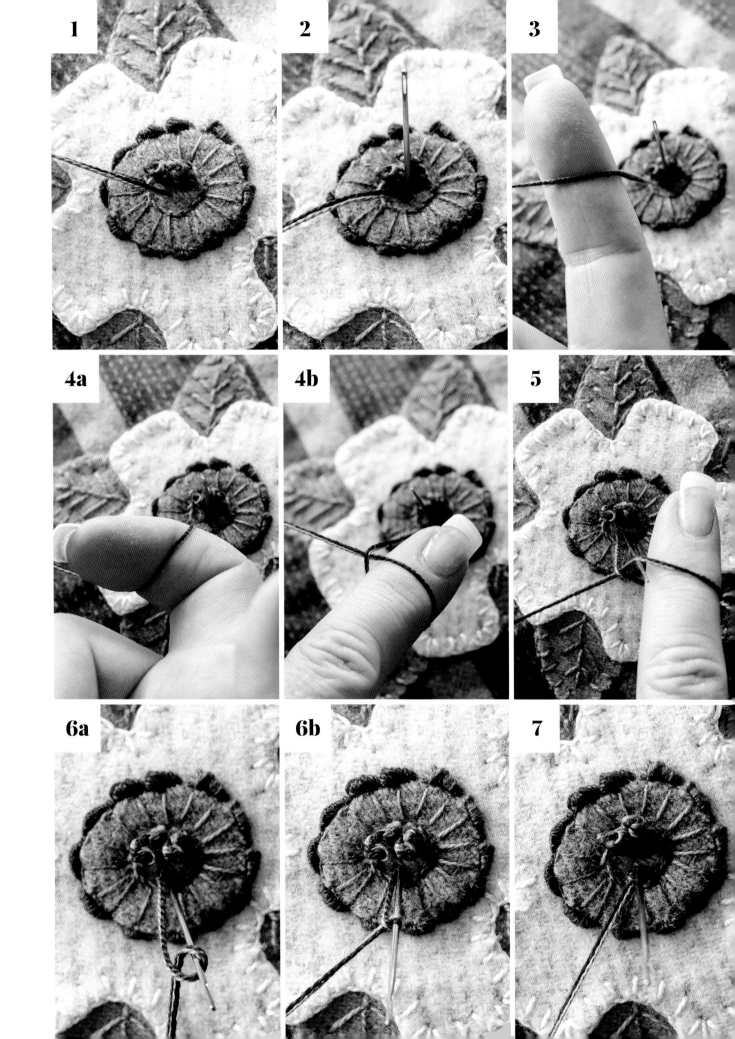

8 Repeat steps 3–7 to add a total of ten loops to the parked needle, sliding each loop to the base as you make it (8). If you're a knitter, this feels a bit like casting on stitches.

9 Rethread the needle without removing it from the pillow (9).

10 Carefully lift your appliqué foundation off the pillow. Hold the working threads taut, with some tension on the needle to prevent the loops from sliding off (10).

11 Slowly pull the threaded needle through the appliqué, keeping tension on the working threads with your thumb (11).

12 Pull the threads completely through to complete a drizzle stitch (12a). The finished stitch will twist like a spiral. Cluster several drizzle stitches together to add dimension to your project (12b).

DAZZLING DRIZZLES

Variegated thread makes beautiful drizzle stitches. If you don't have a variegated thread with the right mix of colors, you can make your own by combining two threads in the needle.

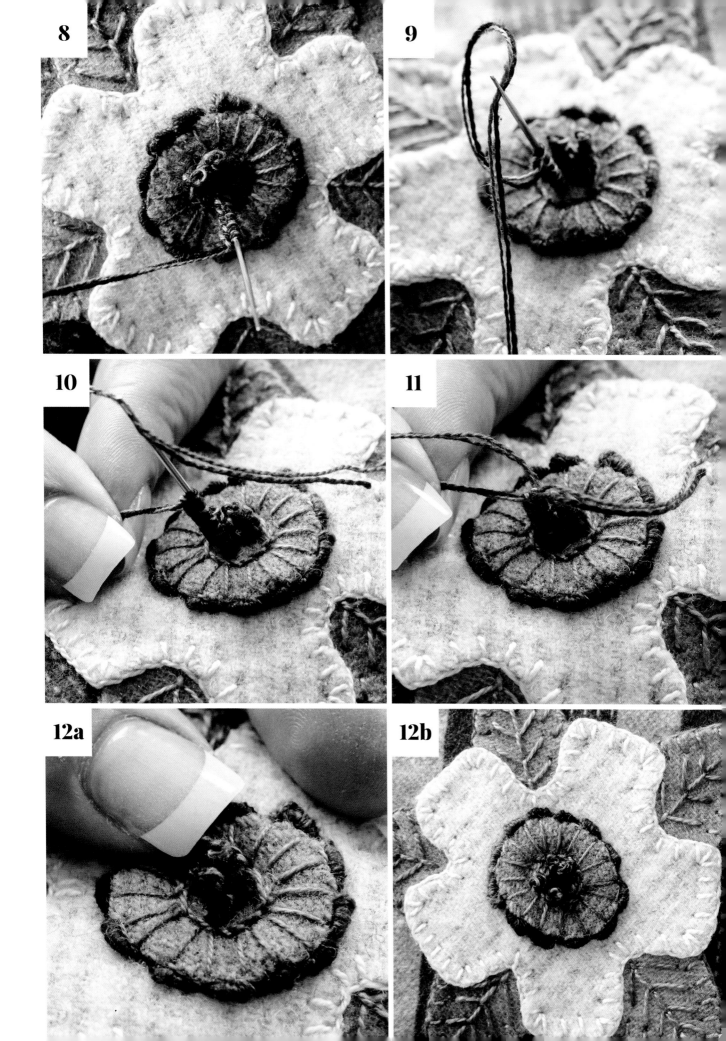

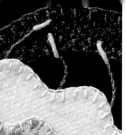

Bullion Stitch

Bullions make a nice edging around appliqué shapes. If you're using the stitch as an edging, stitch into the background just next to the shape, not onto the appliqué shape itself.

1 Bring the threaded needle from the back of the work to the front where you want the end of your first stitch to begin (1); pull the thread through until the knot is against the back.

2 Insert the needle tip where you want the opposite end of your bullion stitch to finish (approximately ¼" away), bringing the tip back up next to the emerging thread (2). Do not pull the needle through; only about half of the needle tip should emerge.

3 Holding the needle steady with your nondominant hand, wrap the working thread clockwise around the tip of the needle as you would for a French knot (3).

4 Repeat wrapping the thread around the needle nine or ten times, keeping it taut, but not so tight you can't later pull the needle through (4).

1

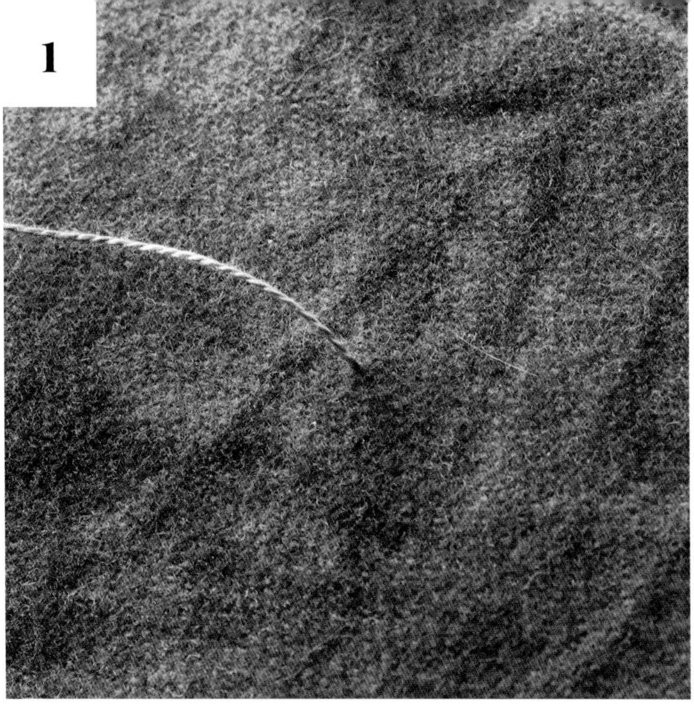

2

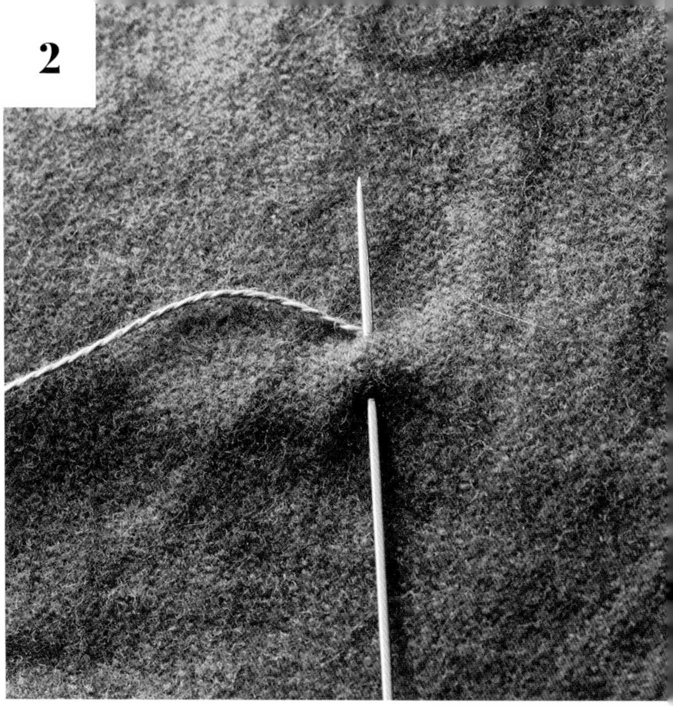

3

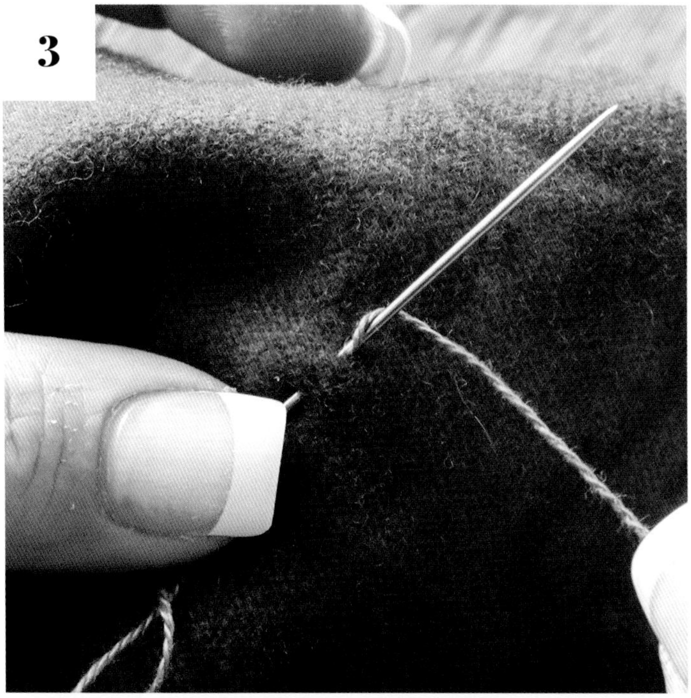

4

A LITTLE KNOW-HOW GOES A LONG WAY

Bullion stitches can be intimidating if you've never made them.
But with a little practice, you'll be whipping through them in no time.
Choosing a needle (I like an embellishing needle) with an even shaft
from eye to tip, rather than a tapered one that is wider at the eye,
will help you pull the needle more smoothly through the bullion.
Consistently wrapping your thread with even tension will also make
it easier to pull the needle through. You'll get the hang of it!

5 Securing the wraps with your left thumb, use your right hand to gently pull the needle through (5a), keeping the working thread coming toward your body, not away from it (5b). Your bullion stitch is completely formed (5c).

6 To end the stitch, insert the needle at the base of the bullion stitch and bring the tip up ¼" above the top end of the bullion where the beginning of your next stitch will be (6). Pull the needle through.

7 Insert the needle tip at the end of the previous bullion stitch, bringing the tip back up next to the emerging thread (7a). Do not pull the needle through; only about half of the needle tip should emerge. Continue as before to make a second bullion stitch (7b).

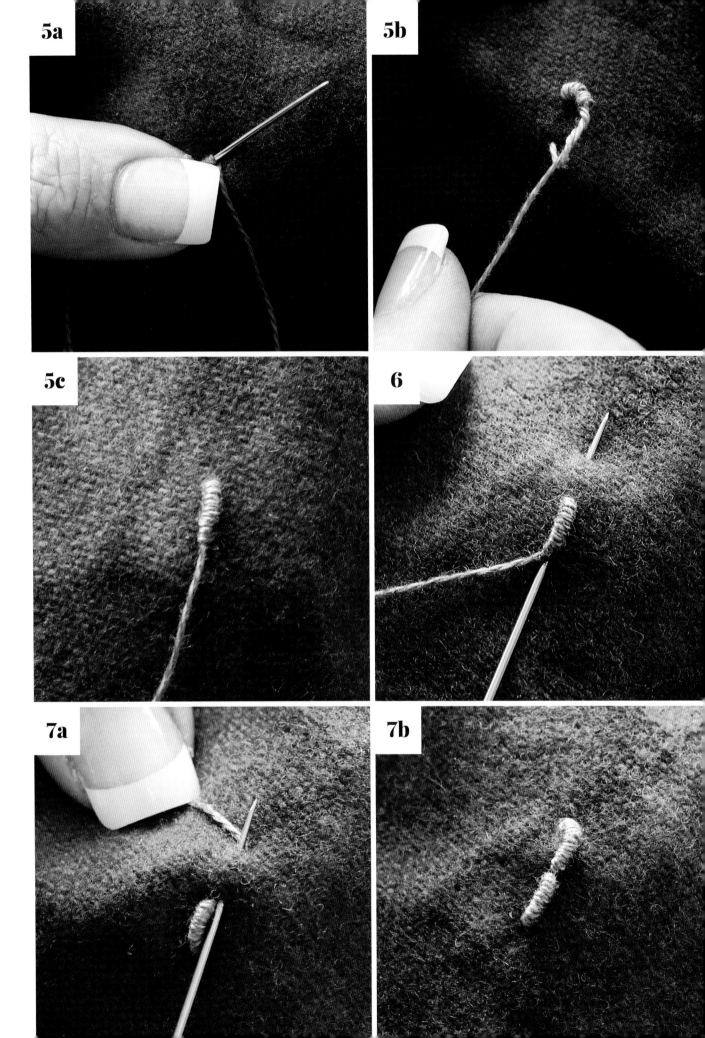

PROJECTS

If you've made it this far, I know you're excited about putting all you've learned into making a project. Lots of stitch books teach you the techniques, but you're left to your own devices to find a project that uses them. Not this book! It's full-service from start to finish. So if you're ready to practice all the parts— from preparing the pieces to finishing the edges—here we go! Choose which project you want to make first (because I know you'll want to make more than one), and let's get stitching!

Geranium Sewing Essentials

MATERIALS

8" × 10" rectangle of straw felted wool for needle book outer cover and lining

8" × 12" rectangle of ecru felted wool for needle book needle page, pot appliqué, and outer scissors holder

4" × 6" rectangle of grand hotel red felted wool for flowers

2" × 4" rectangle of meadow green felted wool for leaves

6½" × 7½" rectangle of ecru cotton print or homespun for scissors holder lining

9" × 16" rectangle of Lite Steam-a-Seam 2 paper-backed fusible web

Valdani #12 pearl cotton: O575 (variegated crispy leaf) and O775 (variegated Turkey red)

Valdani #8 pearl cotton: 1 (black), 4 (ivory), and P5 (variegated vintage tarnished gold)

Chenille needle, size 24

FriXion marking pen

MAKING THE NEEDLE BOOK

Refer to "Stitches" on page 43 for specific stitch details. Work each stitch using the indicated pearl cotton color and the #24 chenille needle.

1. Using the patterns on pages 107–109, refer to "Prepare the Appliqué Shapes" on page 20 to prepare one each of the outer cover/lining and needle page and one pot, 13 leaves, and 19 flowers from the fabrics indicated. Remove the paper backing from all but the outer cover/lining and needle page rectangles.

2. Refer to the photo on page 91 and the appliqué placement diagrams above right to fuse the appliqués to the cover and needle page rectangles. Use the FriXion pen to mark the needle size numbers on the needle page and the decorative detail on the pot. Freehand draw the stems for the dangling flower on the outer cover and the flower on the needle page. Remove the paper backing from the rectangles.

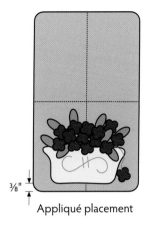 

Appliqué placement   Appliqué placement

3. Using 4, blanket-stitch around the pot.

4. With O575, blanket-stitch around each leaf. Stem-stitch the stem of the dangling flower on the cover and the flower on the needle page.

5. With O775, work four straight stitches over each flower to define the petals, and then make a colonial knot in the center of each flower.

CLEANING YOUR NEEDLE

The exposed fusible web may gum up your needle. If necessary, use a rubbing-alcohol pad to clean the needle.

---

6. With 1, stem-stitch the needle sizes on the needle page and the decorative detail on the pot.

7. Place the outer cover onto the remaining straw wool and fuse it in place using lots of steam. Trim the wool even with the outer cover. Blanket-stitch around the outer edges with P5.

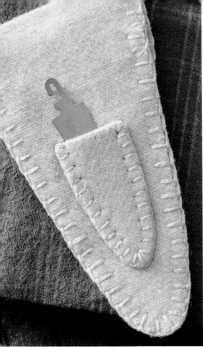
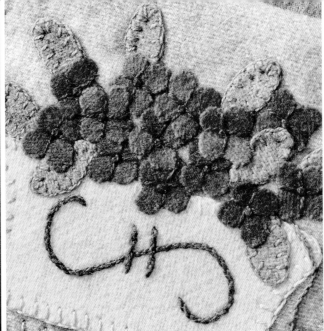

8. Center the needle page on the inside of the cover and fuse it in place. Fly stitch around the page edges with 4, making sure not to stitch through to the right side.

9. Fold the needle book in half, right side out; press the fold using lots of steam. Open the book and load it with #22 and #24 chenille needles.

MAKING THE SCISSORS HOLDER

1. Using the patterns on page 107, refer to "Prepare the Appliqué Shapes" on page 20 to prepare one each of the outer scissors holder, inner scissors holder, and needle threader pocket shapes as well as five leaves and six flowers from the fabrics indicated. Remove the paper backing from all but the outer scissors holder.

2. Refer to the photo on page 91 and the appliqué placement diagram (right) to fuse the appliqués to the scissors holder flap. Remove the paper backing from the outer scissors holder.

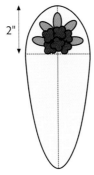

2"

Appliqué placement

3. Blanket-stitch the leaves using O575.

4. With O775, work four straight stitches over each flower to define the petals, and then make a colonial knot in the center of each flower.

5. Fuse the appliquéd outer scissors holder and the wool inner scissors holder to the wrong side of the cotton print rectangle. Trim the cotton fabric even with the wool shapes.

6. Fold the needle threader pocket in half, fusible sides together; fuse. Position the pocket on the outer scissors holder where indicated on the pattern. Using 4, blanket-stitch the pocket in place, starting at the top of the left edge and working to the top of the right edge. Do not stitch across the fold.

7. Place the inner and outer scissors holder shapes with lining sides together. Align the bottom edges. Using a double strand of 4, blanket-stitch across the top edge of the inner shape only. When you reach the side, stitch around the scissors holder through all the layers. I took a couple of extra stitches where the outer and inner pieces meet for added durability, as this is the area that will get the most wear and tear.

8. Slide your tools into their pockets and you're ready to go!

Posey Pincushion

FINISHED SIZE: 4" × 4"

MATERIALS

5" × 10" rectangle of gray stripe flannel for front and
    back

3" × 3" square of cream plaid felted wool for flower

1¼" × 1¼" square of taupe felted wool for flower
    center

2¼" × 5" rectangle of green felted wool for leaves

10" × 10" square of muslin for liner

3" × 6" rectangle of Lite Steam-a-Seam 2
    paper-backed fusible web

Valdani #12 pearl cotton: 4 (ivory), O196 (variegated
    muddy bark), O519 (variegated green olives),
    and O531 (variegated black nut)

Valdani #8 pearl cotton: P4 (vintage light aged white)

Chenille needle, size 24

Clover fine-tip white chalk pen

Clean play sand or filler of choice

CUTTING

From the gray stripe, cut:

2 squares, 4½" × 4½"

From the muslin, cut:

4 squares, 4½" × 4½"

APPLIQUÉING THE PINCUSHION FRONT

Refer to "Stitches" on page 43 for specific stitch
details. Work each stitch using the indicated pearl
cotton color and the size 24 chenille needle.

1. Place the gray stripe squares wrong sides
   together. To round the corners, place a circular
   object on each corner of the top square and
   mark the curve using the white chalk pen. Cut
   on the marked lines through both layers.

 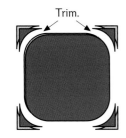

Trim.

2. Refer to "Prepare the Appliqué Shapes" on page
   20 to prepare the appliqué shapes, using the
   patterns on page 109 and the fabrics indicated.

3. Refer to the photo on page 94 and the appliqué
   placement diagram to fuse the appliqués to the
   right side of one gray stripe square.

Appliqué placement

4. Draw a circle ¼" inside the flower center appliqué
   using the white chalk pen. With O196, work a
   blanket stitch around the circle from the outer
   edge to the drawn line. Work bullion stitches
   around the outer edge of the circle using O531.

5. Blanket-stitch around the flower with 4. With
   O519, blanket stitch around the edges of each leaf
   and then work a fly stitch for the leaf detail.

6. With O531, fill the flower center with drizzle
   stitches.

FINISHING THE PINCUSHION

1. Place the four muslin squares together, aligning
   the edges. Stitch around all four sides of the
   layered squares using a ¼" seam allowance,
   leaving an opening along one straight edge to
   insert the sand. Clip the corners and turn the
   squares right side out to create a double-layer
   liner. Fill the liner with sand to the desired
   fullness, then machine stitch the opening closed.

2. Place the appliquéd front and back squares right
   sides together. Stitch ¼" from the edges around
   the square, leaving a large enough opening to
   insert the filled liner. Turn the piece right side out.

3. Insert the liner into the opening; hand stitch the
   opening closed.

4. Using P4, work a fly stitch over the seamline.

White Geraniums Table Mat

FINISHED SIZE: 15" round

MATERIALS

16" × 16" square of silo felted wool for background

5" × 5" square of ecru felted wool for flowers

6" × 8" rectangle of terra-cotta felted wool for flowerpots and rims

5" × 5" square of Santa's beard felted wool for leaves

1 fat quarter (18" × 21") of coordinating homespun for backing

16" × 24" rectangle of Lite Steam-a-Seam 2 paper-backed fusible web

Valdani #8 pearl cotton: O126 (old cottage grey)

Valdani #12 pearl cotton: 148 (luminous beige), M49 (subtle elegance), and O153 (coffee roast)

Chenille needle, size 24

Clover fine-tip white chalk pen

MAKING THE TABLE MAT

Refer to "Stitches" on page 43 for specific stitch details. Work each stitch using the indicated pearl cotton color and the size 24 chenille needle.

1. Refer to "Prepare the Appliqué Background" on page 16. Use the quarter background pattern on page 110 to make a complete background.

2. Refer to "Prepare the Appliqué Shapes" on page 20 to prepare the appliqué shapes, using the patterns on page 111 and the fabrics indicated.

3. Fuse flowerpots and rims to the background. With 1 strand of O153, blanket-stitch each piece.

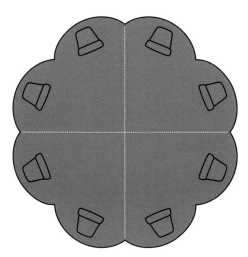

Appliqué placement

4. Using the white chalk pen, draw the stem of each flower. Stem-stitch each stem using two strands of 148.

5. Position the leaves on each stem and fuse them in place. Blanket-stitch around each one using one strand of 148.

6. Arrange 10 flowers at the top of each stem in a pleasing cluster; fuse in place. Using one strand of M49, work four straight stitches on each flower. Using two strands of M49, make a colonial or French knot in the center of each flower.

7. Refer to "Finishing the Project Edge" on page 30 to complete the table mat, using the homespun for the backing and one strand of O126 to blanket-stitch the edges.

2019 Pincushion

FINISHED SIZE: 4½" × 9½"

MATERIALS

11" × 11" square of gray check flannel for front and back

3" × 5" rectangle of ecru felted wool for flowers

3" × 3" square of pistachio felted wool for leaves

½" × 7" strip of taupe felted wool for stem

1 fat quarter (18" × 21") of muslin for liner

3½" × 4" rectangle of Lite Steam-a-Seam 2 paper-backed fusible web

Valdani #8 and #12 pearl cotton: P4 (vintage light aged white)

Chenille needle, size 24

Clover fine-tip white chalk pen

Clean play sand

CUTTING

From the gray check flannel, cut:

2 rectangles, 5" × 10"

From the muslin, cut:

4 rectangles, 5" × 10"

MAKING THE PINCUSHION FRONT

Refer to "Stitches" on page 43 for specific stitch details. Work each stitch using the indicated pearl cotton weight and the size 24 chenille needle.

1. Refer to "Prepare the Appliqué Shapes" on page 20 to prepare the appliqué shapes, using the patterns on page 111 and the fabrics indicated. Refer to "Make Stems" on page 22 to make a ³⁄₁₆" × 7" stem from the taupe wool.

2. Refer to the photo on page 98 and the appliqué and embroidery placement diagram to fuse the appliqués to the right side of one gray rectangle. Use the white chalk pen to freehand mark the date on the rectangle.

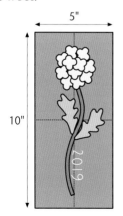

Appliqué placement

3. Using #12 pearl cotton, work a cross-stitch over the stem. Blanket-stitch the edges of each leaf and then stem-stitch the leaf details. Stem-stitch the date with #8 pearl cotton. Add your initials as I did, if desired.

4. With a single strand of #8 pearl cotton, work four straight stitches over each flower to define the petals, and then use a double strand to make a colonial knot in the center of each flower.

FINISHING THE PINCUSHION

1. Place the four muslin rectangles together, aligning the edges. Stitch around all four sides of the layered rectangles using a ¼" seam allowance, leaving an opening along any side to insert the sand. Clip the corners and turn the rectangles right side out to create a double-layer liner. Fill the liner with sand to the desired fullness, and then machine stitch the opening closed.

2. Place the appliquéd front and back rectangles right sides together. Stitch ¼" from the edges around the rectangles, leaving a large enough opening along the long edge to insert the filled liner. Turn the piece right side out.

3. Insert the liner into the opening, and then hand stitch the opening closed.

Autumn Table Mat

FINISHED SIZE: 22" round

MATERIALS

23" × 23" square of stone wool for background

4" × 8" rectangle of chocolate wool for small and large acorns, crow branches, and owl branch

2" × 5" rectangle of raven wool for owl head and body

1" × 3" rectangle of cow patty wool for pumpkin stems

4" × 5" rectangle of pumpkin plaid wool for pumpkin A and pumpkin B center

3" × 7" rectangle of black stripe wool for owl wings and crow B body

3" × 7" rectangle of black wool for crow A body and crow B wings

2" × 3" rectangle of dark chocolate wool for sunflower center

2½" × 3" rectangle of black mini-plaid wool for small and large acorn caps

2½" × 3½" rectangle of pumpkin wool for pumpkin B

1¼" × 3" rectangle of black plaid wool for crow A wing

3½" × 5" rectangle of caramel wool for sunflower and moon

3½" × 3½" square of toffee wool for squirrel

4" × 4" square *each* of autumn leaf, forest, saltbox, and brown leaf wools for leaves

23" × 23" square of tan homespun for backing

24" × 36" rectangle of Lite Steam-a-Seam 2 paper-backed fusible web

Valdani #12 pearl cotton: 1 (black), 1645 (dark red brown), M90 (variegated chocolate brownies), O78 (variegated deep burgundy), O154 (variegated dark antique golds), O178 (variegated tea-dyed stone), O548 (variegated blackened khaki), and P12 (variegated vintage browns)

Valdani #8 pearl cotton: O510 (variegated terra-cotta), O196 (variegated muddy bark), and P12 (variegated vintage browns)

Chenille needle, size 24

Clover fine-tip white chalk pen

FriXion marking pen, brown

MAKING THE TABLE MAT

1. Refer to "Prepare the Appliqué Background" on page 16 and use the one-eighth background pattern on page 106 to prepare a complete background shape.

2. Refer to "Prepare the Appliqué Shapes" on page 20 to prepare the appliqué shapes, using patterns on pages 103–105 and fabrics indicated.

3. Refer to the photo on page 100 and the appliqué placement diagram to fuse the appliqués to the background.

Appliqué placement

4. Using #12 pearl cotton and referring to "Stitches" on page 43 for specific stitch details, follow the thread and stitch chart on page 102 to blanket-stitch around each appliqué, and then add any detail stitching.

5. Using the FriXion pen, freehand draw the bittersweet vine lines connecting the appliqué shapes, referring to the photo on page 100 as needed. With #8 pearl cotton in P12, stem stitch the lines. Add colonial or French knot berries to the ends of the lines with O510.

6. Refer to "Finishing the Project Edge" on page 30 to complete the table mat, using the tan homespun for the backing and #8 pearl cotton in O196 for the blanket stitch.

AUTUMN TABLE MAT THREAD AND STITCH CHART

PUMPKIN #1

Appliqué Piece	Stitch Used	Thread Color
Pumpkin	Blanket	M90
Stem	Blanket	P12
Leaves	Blanket	1645
Leaf detail	Stem	1645
Pumpkin detail	Stem	M90

PUMPKIN #2

Appliqué Piece	Stitch Used	Thread Color
Pumpkin	Blanket	M90
Stem	Blanket	P12
Leaves	Blanket	1645
Leaf detail	Stem	1645

CROW #1

Appliqué Piece	Stitch Used	Thread Color
Crow	Blanket	1
Wing	Blanket	1
Eye	French knot	1
Wing detail	Fly	M90
Branch	Cross	1645

CROW #2

Appliqué Piece	Stitch Used	Thread Color
Crow	Blanket	1
Wing	Blanket	1
Eye	French knot	1
Wing detail	Fly	1645
Branch	Cross	P12

SUNFLOWER

Appliqué Piece	Stitch Used	Thread Color
Sunflower	Blanket	O154
Center	Blanket	1645
Leaves	Blanket	1645
Leaf detail	Stem	1645

SQUIRREL

Appliqué Piece	Stitch Used	Thread Color
Body	Blanket	P9
Small acorn cap	Blanket	1
Small acorn	Blanket	P12
Acorn stem	Straight	1
Leg detail	Stem	P9
Eye	French knot	1
Ear details	Straight	1

ACORN

Appliqué Piece	Stitch Used	Thread Color
Large acorn cap	Blanket	1
Large acorn	Blanket	1645
Leaves	Blanket	O548
Leaf detail	Stem	1645

OWL

Appliqué Piece	Stitch Used	Thread Color
Body	Blanket	P12
Head	Blanket	P12
Wings	Blanket	H212
Wing detail	Feather	H212
Branch	Cross	1645
Iris	Stem	O178
Pupil	French knot	1
Moon	Blanket	O154
Beak	Satin	O154

PATTERNS

AUTUMN TABLE MAT page 100

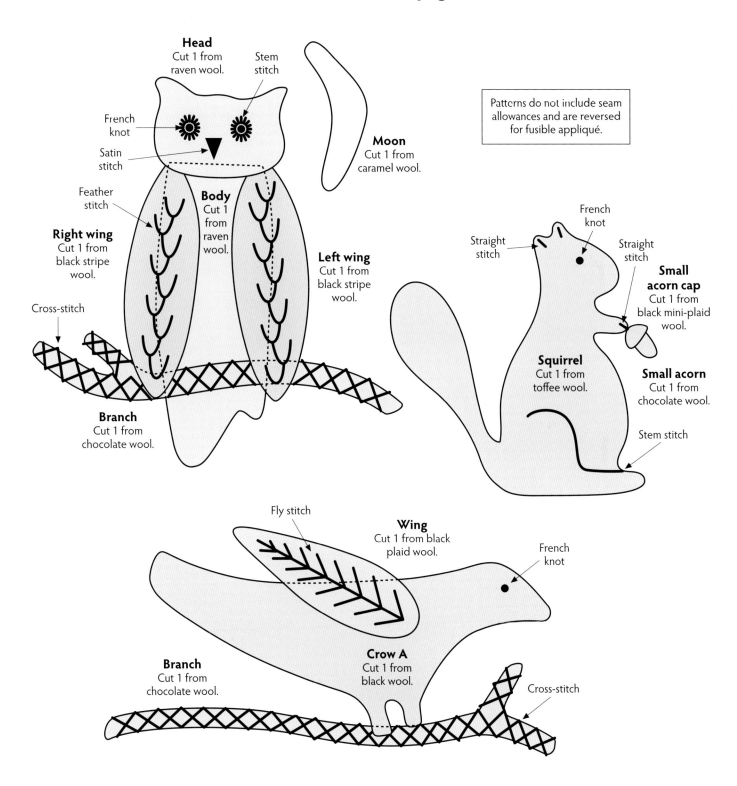

Head
Cut 1 from raven wool.

Stem stitch

French knot

Satin stitch

Feather stitch

Right wing
Cut 1 from black stripe wool.

Cross-stitch

Branch
Cut 1 from chocolate wool.

Body
Cut 1 from raven wool.

Left wing
Cut 1 from black stripe wool.

Moon
Cut 1 from caramel wool.

Patterns do not include seam allowances and are reversed for fusible appliqué.

French knot

Straight stitch

Straight stitch

Small acorn cap
Cut 1 from black mini-plaid wool.

Squirrel
Cut 1 from toffee wool.

Small acorn
Cut 1 from chocolate wool.

Stem stitch

Fly stitch

Wing
Cut 1 from black plaid wool.

French knot

Branch
Cut 1 from chocolate wool.

Crow A
Cut 1 from black wool.

Cross-stitch

AUTUMN TABLE MAT page 100

Patterns do not include seam allowances and are reversed for fusible appliqué.

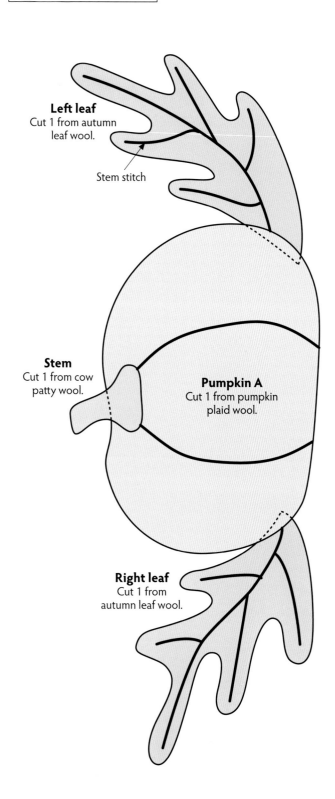

Left leaf
Cut 1 from autumn leaf wool.

Stem stitch

Stem
Cut 1 from cow patty wool.

Pumpkin A
Cut 1 from pumpkin plaid wool.

Right leaf
Cut 1 from autumn leaf wool.

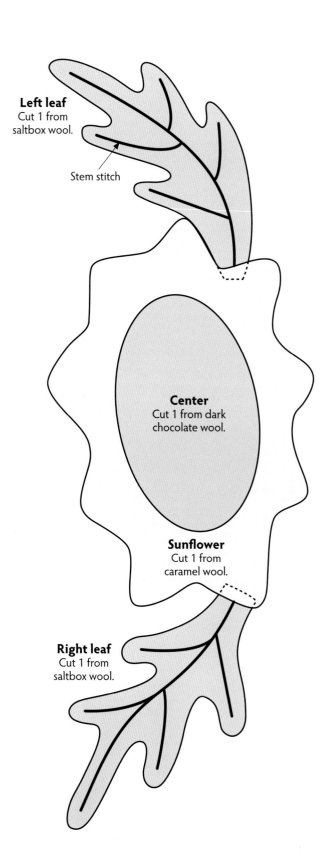

Left leaf
Cut 1 from saltbox wool.

Stem stitch

Center
Cut 1 from dark chocolate wool.

Sunflower
Cut 1 from caramel wool.

Right leaf
Cut 1 from saltbox wool.

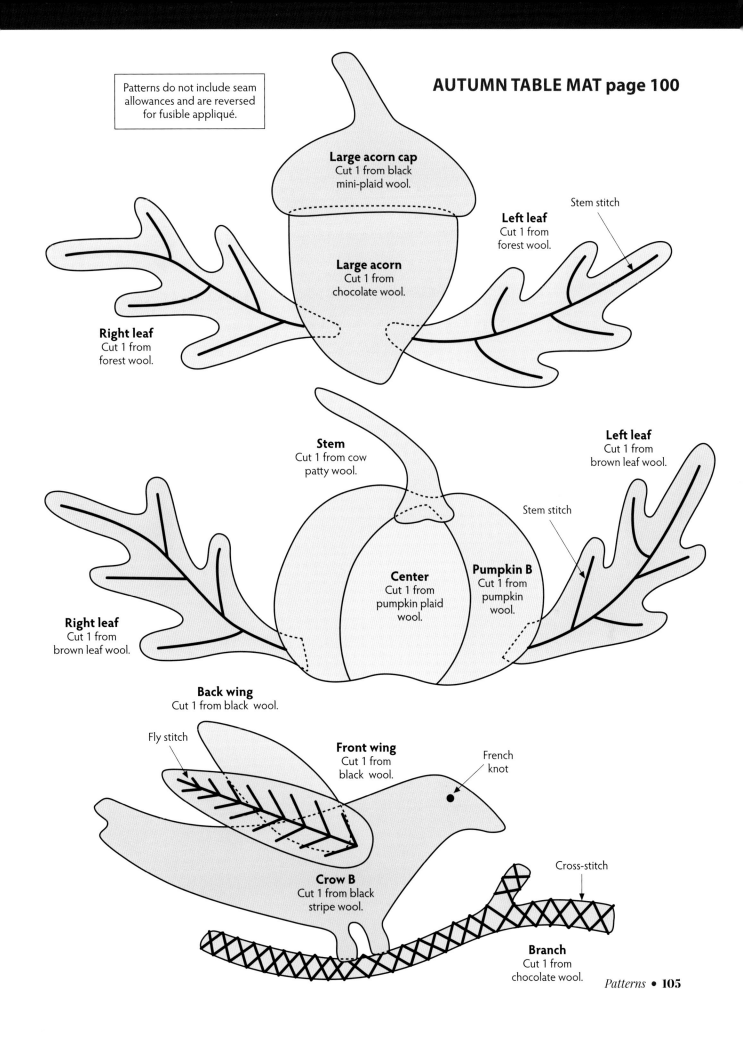

Patterns do not include seam allowances and are reversed for fusible appliqué.

Large acorn cap
Cut 1 from black mini-plaid wool.

Stem stitch

Left leaf
Cut 1 from forest wool.

Large acorn
Cut 1 from chocolate wool.

Right leaf
Cut 1 from forest wool.

Stem
Cut 1 from cow patty wool.

Left leaf
Cut 1 from brown leaf wool.

Stem stitch

Center
Cut 1 from pumpkin plaid wool.

Pumpkin B
Cut 1 from pumpkin wool.

Right leaf
Cut 1 from brown leaf wool.

Back wing
Cut 1 from black wool.

Fly stitch

Front wing
Cut 1 from black wool.

French knot

Crow B
Cut 1 from black stripe wool.

Cross-stitch

Branch
Cut 1 from chocolate wool.

Patterns • **105**

AUTUMN TABLE MAT page 100

1. Prepare a piece of gridded fusible webbing at least 22" × 22".

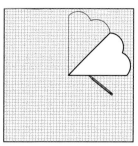

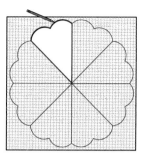

2. Trace one-eighth background template onto gridded side of fusible web. Rotate 45° and align straight edge. Trace a second time.

3. Continue tracing to complete pattern.

**Autumn Table Mat
one-eighth background
pattern**

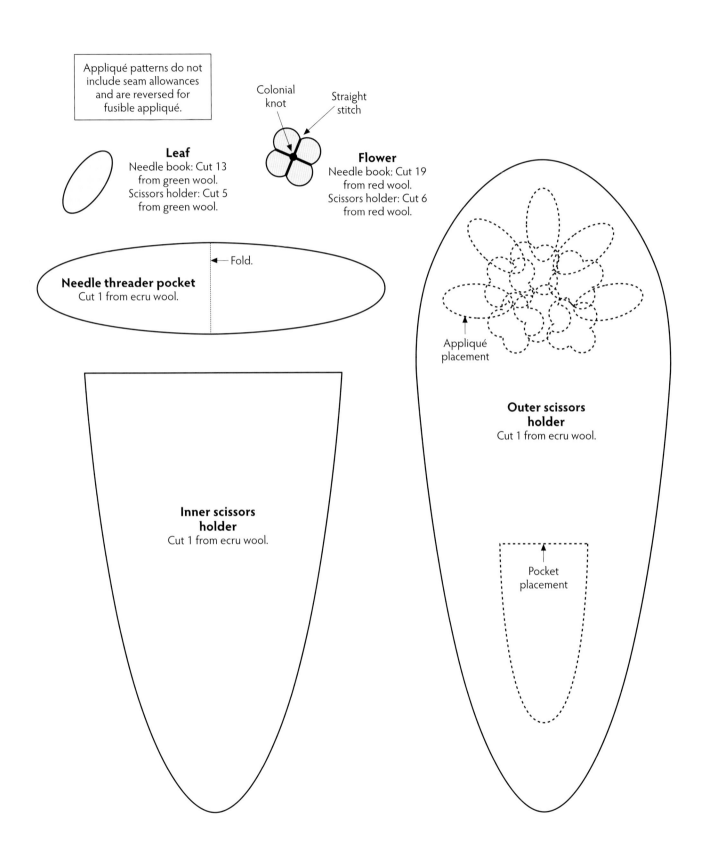

Appliqué patterns do not include seam allowances and are reversed for fusible appliqué.

Leaf
Needle book: Cut 13 from green wool.
Scissors holder: Cut 5 from green wool.

Colonial knot

Straight stitch

Flower
Needle book: Cut 19 from red wool.
Scissors holder: Cut 6 from red wool.

← Fold.

Needle threader pocket
Cut 1 from ecru wool.

Appliqué placement

Outer scissors holder
Cut 1 from ecru wool.

Inner scissors holder
Cut 1 from ecru wool.

Pocket placement

GERANIUM SEWING ESSENTIALS page 91

Pattern does not include seam allowances and is reversed for fusible appliqué.

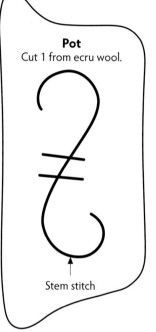

Pot
Cut 1 from ecru wool.

Stem stitch

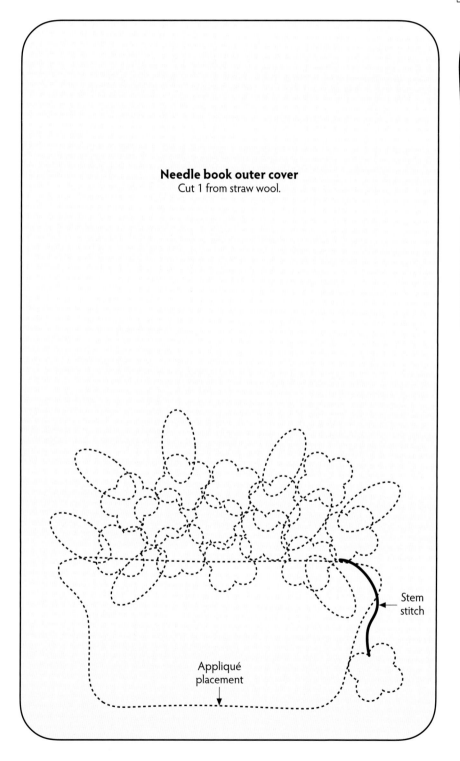

Needle book outer cover
Cut 1 from straw wool.

Stem stitch

Appliqué placement

GERANIUM SEWING ESSENTIALS page 91

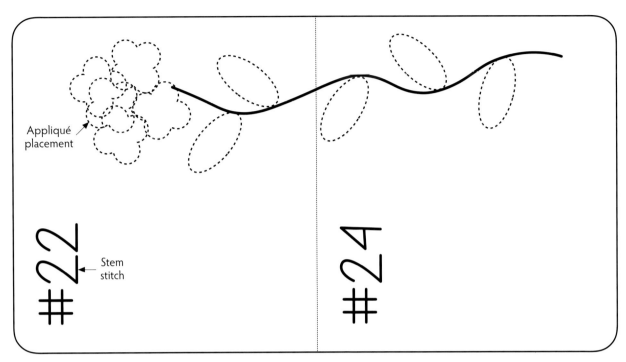

Appliqué placement

#22

Stem stitch

#24

Needle page
Cut 1 from ecru wool.

POSEY PINCUSHION page 94

Patterns do not include seam allowances and are reversed for fusible appliqué.

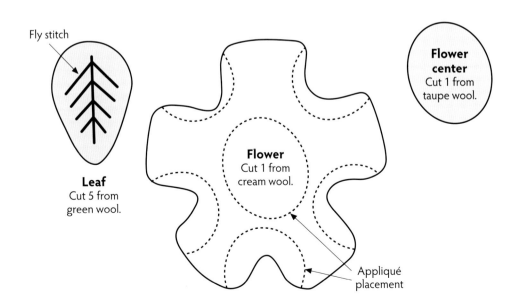

Fly stitch

Leaf
Cut 5 from green wool.

Flower
Cut 1 from cream wool.

Flower center
Cut 1 from taupe wool.

Appliqué placement

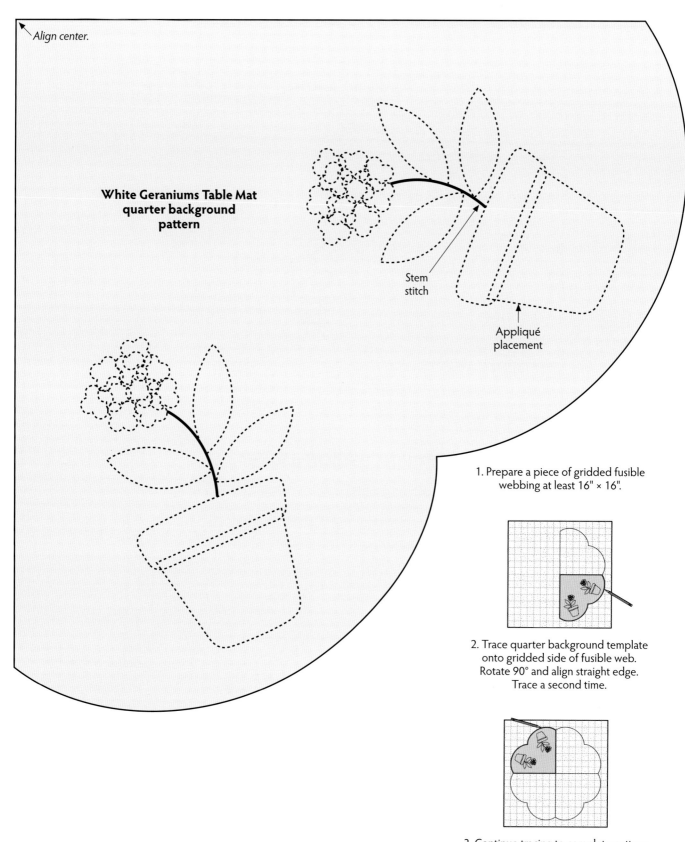

Align center.

**White Geraniums Table Mat
quarter background
pattern**

Stem
stitch

Appliqué
placement

1. Prepare a piece of gridded fusible
webbing at least 16" × 16".

2. Trace quarter background template
onto gridded side of fusible web.
Rotate 90° and align straight edge.
Trace a second time.

3. Continue tracing to complete pattern.

WHITE GERANIUMS TABLE MAT page 96

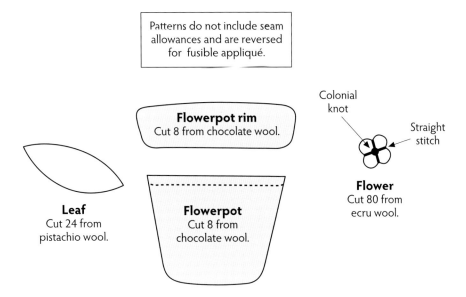

Patterns do not include seam allowances and are reversed for fusible appliqué.

Flowerpot rim
Cut 8 from chocolate wool.

Colonial knot

Straight stitch

Flower
Cut 80 from ecru wool.

Leaf
Cut 24 from pistachio wool.

Flowerpot
Cut 8 from chocolate wool.

2019 PINCUSHION page 98

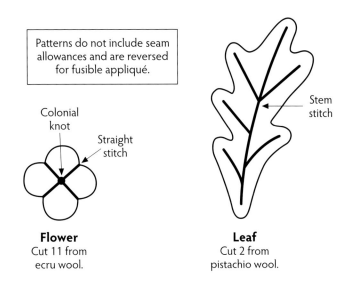

Patterns do not include seam allowances and are reversed for fusible appliqué.

Colonial knot

Straight stitch

Flower
Cut 11 from ecru wool.

Stem stitch

Leaf
Cut 2 from pistachio wool.

ABOUT THE AUTHOR

You can't be around designer Lisa Bongean for long without picking up her infectious enthusiasm for stitching, both by hand and by machine. But if pressed, she'll probably tell you her heart is with wool stitchery. The combination of richly textured wools, delightfully colorful threads, and the endless array of shapes that you can cut—she's a fan of it all! Which is probably why she's been a teacher to so many stitchers over the years. There's little that she hasn't tried, and so much that she's learned and is willing to share. She's matter-of-fact about the tools and supplies she likes to use and why. If practice, practice, practice is the key to getting it right, it's clear that's why Lisa Bongean's a leader in the wool stitchery world. Her workmanship is impeccable because she never stops making more.

The owner of Primitive Gatherings (PrimitiveGatherings.us), Lisa has shops in both Menasha, Wisconsin, and Murrieta, California, that specialize in hand-dyed wools, quilting cottons, and kits. And the book you're holding is her dream come true—the chance to share her love of wool, needle, and thread with others in the hope that they'll love it too.